Sweet Success

by Wendy Godfrey

Golden Press · New York
Western Publishing Company, Inc.
Racine, Wisconsin

Introduction

A beautiful big book devoted totally to sweets.
Many are traditional English favorites, like Bakewell Tarts and Eccles Cakes.
Others, like Doughnuts and Candy Apples on a Stick,
we tend to think of as uniquely American.
Every recipe has been "translated" for American cooks and every recipe's
ingredients are given in both standard American measurements
and metric measurements.
Please use only one type of measurement at a time –
never mix the two in one recipe.

Let your eyes feast on the glorious pictures.
Then let the rest of you feast in a different way.
To your Sweet Success!

Sweets & Things

Sugar Mice, Candy Apples on a Stick, Honeycomb Toffee, Rum Truffles, Chocolate Cups,
French Nougat.
Butterscotch, Marshmallows, Butterscotch Fudge, Chocolate & Walnut Fudge.
Peppermint Ice, Crème de Menthe, Turkish Delight, Marrons Glacé, Fruit Jellies.
Barley Sugar, Praline, Russian Caramels, Grapes in Caramel, Marzipan Petit Fours.
Coconut Kisses, Coconut Ice, Lemon Squash, Iced Summer Punch, Mulled Punch, Apple Beer.
Mocha Sauce, Frothy Chocolate, Crème à la Vanille, Foamy Orange Sauce.
Coffee Frosting, Brandy Butter, Butterscotch Sauce.

Cakes & Cookies

Doughnuts, Old-fashioned Jumbles, Coffee Gingerbread, Canadian Gingerbread.
Japanese Cakes, Mincemeat Shortbread, Bath Buns, Selkirk Bannocks, Ann's Coconut
Cookies.
Cinnamon Toast, Treacle Scones, Golden Oatcakes, Feather Iced Cakes.
Spiced Raspberry Buns, Easter Cookies, Swedish Tea Ring, Vanilla Slice.
Apricot Tea Bread, Nutty Meringues, Banana Nut Bread, Danish Pastries.
Walnut Layer Cake with American Frosting, Marshmallow Crispies, Lardy Cake.
Bakewell Tart, Madeleines, Eccles Cakes, Refrigerator Cookies.
Genoese Fancies, Chocolate Nests, Simnel Cake, Hearts & Flowers Cake.

Preserves

Banana Jam, Gooseberry & Elderflower Jelly, Mustard Pickle, Bread & Butter Relish.
Ripe Tomato Chutney, Apple & Raisin Chutney, Plum Chutney, Orchard Marmalade.
Tangerine Marmalade, Orange Jelly Marmalade, Whiskey Marmalade.
Rhubarb Ginger Jam, Quince Jelly, Grapefruit Curd, Dried Apricot Jam, Apple Butter.
Melon & Ginger Jam, Strawberry Conserve, Candied Peel, Fruit & Nut Conserve.
Mincemeat, Spiced Clementines, Pickled Pears, Pears in Brandy, Potent Prunes.
Sage Jelly, Dried Apple Rings, Crystallized Flowers, Raspberry Freezer Jam.
Raspberry Vinegar, Syrup for Freezing, Tomato Sauce.

Puddings

Gateau Amandine, Crème Brûlée, Wholemeal Treacle Tart, Lincoln Tart.
Chestnut Parfait, French Apple Flan, Spotted Richard, Pancakes, Claret Jelly.
Bananas Trinidad, Lemon Surprise Pudding, Meringue Baskets.
Apricot and Almond Charlotte, Caramelized Oranges, Pineapple Upside-Down Cake.
Peach Condé, Gateau St. Honoré, Strawberry Soufflé, Toffee Apple Pudding.
Rhubarb & Orange Fool, Blackberry Mousse, Whiskey & Oatmeal Syllabub.
Raspberry Mousse Mold, Sussex Pond Pudding, Mincemeat & Apple Jalousie.
Baked Ginger Pears, Lemon & Grape Cheesecake, Praline Ice Cream, Rum Stockade.
Swiss Apple, Brown Bread Pudding, Butterscotch Meringue Pie.

Sweets & Things

Sugar Mice

Sugar mice can be used to decorate a party table anytime. At Christmas they make charming stocking stuffers.

Preparation time: 30 minutes

4 cups (1 lb.)/500 g confectioners' sugar. 1 egg white. 2 tablespoons/50 g light corn syrup. Food color (optional). String. Large silver dragées or cinnamon red-hots. Cornstarch.

Sift 3 cups of the confectioners' sugar into a bowl. Add the egg white and the corn syrup and mix with a wooden spoon. Gradually add the remaining confectioners' sugar and work in until the mixture is the consistency of pastry dough. Food color may be added and kneaded into the mixture if desired. Shape into mice, add ears made from the same sugar mixture, a string tail and two silver dragées or red-hots for eyes.

Place completed mice on waxed paper sprinkled with cornstarch and allow to dry.

Candy Apples on a stick

Old-fashioned candy apples are a favorite fall treat and will quickly sell at fund-raising events.

Preparation and cooking time: 30 minutes

12 medium-size eating apples. Wooden skewers. ½ cup/150 g light corn syrup. 1½ cups/300 g light brown sugar. 2 tablespoons/25 g butter. ⅔ cup/150 ml water. 1 teaspoon/5 ml vinegar.

Wash and dry the apples thoroughly. Remove the stems and stick a wooden skewer into the stem end of each apple. Combine all the other ingredients in a large, heavy saucepan and stir over low heat until the sugar dissolves. Continue cooking until candy thermometer reads 290° F or a small amount of syrup dropped into cold water indicates the hard-crack stage. Remove pan from heat and, working fast, dip each apple into the syrup, twisting skewer so that fruit is completely coated. Dip each apple in cold water and place on a well-greased cookie sheet for candy to harden. Because candy apples become sticky from exposure to the atmosphere, they should be wrapped if they are not going to be eaten immediately.

Honeycomb Toffee

Honeycomb toffee is called "cinder toffee"
in some parts of northern England.
Preparation and cooking time: 30 minutes

¾ cup/250 g light corn syrup. 2 cups/500 g sugar. ⅓ cup/60 g butter.
1 teaspoon/5 ml vinegar. 5 tablespoons/75 ml water.
2 teaspoons/10 ml baking soda.

Put all the ingredients except the baking soda into a large, heavy
saucepan. Cook slowly until the sugar dissolves. Continue cooking
until candy thermometer reads 290° F or a small amount of syrup
dropped into cold water indicates the hard-crack stage. Remove pan
from heat and add the baking soda. The mixture will bubble,
producing a honeycomb texture. Pour into a buttered 8-inch square
pan. Mark into squares when half-cool; break off squares when cold.

Rum Truffles

Sophisticated rum-flavored chocolates make
the perfect ending to a dinner party.
Preparation and cooking time: 30 minutes

1 cup (6 oz.)/150 g semisweet chocolate pieces. 2 egg yolks.
2 tablespoons/25 g butter. 2 teaspoons/10 ml heavy cream.
1 tablespoon/15 ml rum. 2 cups/225 g confectioners' sugar.
Chocolate sprinkles.

Melt the chocolate pieces over hot water. Remove from heat and add
the yolks, butter, cream and rum. Gradually work in the confectioners'
sugar until the mixture just holds together. Roll into small balls and
coat each with chocolate sprinkles. Allow to set on waxed paper.
Makes about 1 pound.

Chocolate Cups

These are delicious served with coffee after a meal. Almonds or
walnuts could be substituted for the pistachio nuts.
Preparation time: 1 hour

4 squares (1 oz. each)/100 g unsweetened chocolate.
Paper wrappers for bite-size chocolates.
4 squares (1 oz. each)/100 g semisweet chocolate or
⅔ cup semisweet chocolate pieces.
1 cup/100 g confectioners' sugar. Rum. Chopped pistachio nuts.

Melt the unsweetened chocolate over hot water. Pour a little of the
melted chocolate into each paper candy wrapper and run it around the
inside to form a cup. Place in the refrigerator until set. Carefully peel
off the paper. Melt the semisweet chocolate over hot water; remove
from heat. Sift confectioners' sugar and beat into melted chocolate,
adding enough rum to give the mixture a soft, creamy consistency.
Pipe or spoon the rum mixture into the cups and sprinkle the tops
with chopped pistachio nuts. Makes about 20 cups.

FRENCH NOUGAT

This is very authentic-tasting nougat and makes a charming gift,
packed into pretty boxes.
Preparation and cooking time: 45-60 minutes

Parchment paper. ¾ cup/100 g whole blanched almonds.
2 cups/450 g granulated sugar.
2 cups/225 g confectioners' sugar. ⅔ cup/150 ml water.
2 egg whites. ½ cup (2 oz.)/50 g chopped angelica.
⅓ cup/50 g chopped candied red cherries.

Line an 8-inch-square pan with parchment paper. (If not available,
butter pan and sprinkle with confectioners' sugar.) Brown the almonds
in the oven and chop coarsely. Heat the granulated sugar,
confectioners' sugar and water in a large, heavy pan until the sugars
dissolve, and then boil until candy thermometer reads 270° F or a few
drops of syrup dropped into cold water indicate the soft-crack stage.
Beat the egg whites until stiff and gradually add the syrup. Keep
beating until the mixture thickens. (This may take up to 30 minutes
but it is important if the nougat is going to set.) Add the almonds,
angelica and cherries. Mix well and pour into the prepared pan. Cover
with parchment paper (or brown paper sprinkled with confectioners'
sugar) and press down with a weight. Set aside for 12 hours and then
cut into squares.
Makes about 1½ pounds.

■Butterscotch

Mouthwatering butterscotch – as much fun to make as to eat!
Preparation and cooking time: 30 minutes

3 cups/600 g brown sugar. ⅔ cup/150 ml water. ¼ cup/60 g butter.

Butter an 8-inch-square pan. Dissolve the sugar in the water in a
large, heavy saucepan over medium heat. Then, without stirring, bring
to a boil and cook until candy thermometer reads 280° F or a few
drops of syrup dropped into cold water indicate the soft-crack stage.
Stir in the butter a little at a time. Pour into the pan
and mark into squares when cool.

▯MARSHMALLOWS

Delicately textured pink and white sweets to make for special gifts.
Preparation and cooking time: 30-45 minutes

2 cups/450 g granulated sugar.
1 tablespoon/25 g light corn syrup. 1½ cups/300 ml water.
2 envelopes (1 tablespoon each)/30 ml unflavored gelatin.
2 egg whites. ½ teaspoon/2.5 ml vanilla. Red food color.
Cornstarch. Confectioners' sugar.

Put the granulated sugar, corn syrup and half the water into a large,
heavy pan. Dissolve sugar over low heat and then bring to a boil and
continue cooking until candy thermometer reads 260° F or a few
drops of mixture dropped into cold water indicate the soft-crack stage.
While mixture is boiling, soak the gelatin in remaining water. Remove
syrup pan from heat and add gelatin mixture. Stir until dissolved. Beat
the egg whites and pour on the hot syrup in a thin stream, beating all
the while. Add vanilla and a drop or two of red color and continue
beating until the mixture is thick and stiff. Pour into a 9-inch-square
pan lined with greased waxed paper and let stand exposed to the air
for at least 24 hours. Remove from the pan and cut into squares. Roll
each piece thoroughly in a mixture of 1 part cornstarch and 2 parts
confectioners' sugar. Store in an airtight container.

▯ Butterscotch Fudge

Chopped seedless raisins or nuts may be added to the fudge.
Preparation and cooking time: 30 minutes

2 cups/450 g sugar. ⅔ cup/150 ml evaporated milk. ¼ cup/50 g butter.
3 tablespoons/45 ml water. ⅔ cup/150 ml milk.
1 teaspoon/5 ml butterscotch flavor.

Put all the ingredients except butterscotch flavor into a large, heavy
saucepan. Stir over low heat until the sugar dissolves and then bring
to a boil and cook until candy thermometer reads 240° F or a bit of
the mixture dropped into cold water indicates the soft-ball stage. Add
the butterscotch flavor and beat well until the mixture thickens and
feels grainy. Spread in buttered shallow pan. Score while warm; cut
into squares when firm.

■ Chocolate and Walnut Fudge

For an extra festive touch, place a walnut half on each square before the fudge has completely set.

Preparation and cooking time: 20 minutes

4 squares (1 oz. each)/100 g semisweet chocolate
or ⅔ cup semisweet chocolate pieces.
2 teaspoons/10 ml instant coffee powder. ¼ cup/50 g butter.
4 tablespoons/60 ml light cream.
1 teaspoon/5 ml vanilla. ½ cup/50 g coarsely chopped walnuts.
4 cups (approximately 1 lb.)/450 g confectioners' sugar.

Place the chocolate, coffee powder and butter in top of a double boiler and stir over hot water until chocolate is melted. Remove from heat and stir in the cream and vanilla. Add nuts. Sift the sugar and work into chocolate mixture. Spread in a buttered 8-inch-square pan. Smooth top and put in a cool place. When firm, cut into squares. Makes about 1½ pounds.

PEPPERMINT ICE

A smooth and creamy confection with a refreshing flavor.
Preparation and cooking time: 20 minutes

2 cups/500 g sugar. ⅔ cup/150 ml water.
1 teaspoon/5 ml peppermint extract. Green food color.

Put sugar and water into a heavy saucepan and stir over low heat until the sugar dissolves. Boil gently without stirring until candy thermometer reads 245° F or a bit of the mixture dropped into cold water indicates the firm-ball stage. Remove pan from heat and add peppermint extract and a drop or two of food color. Pour into an oiled 8-inch-square pan and allow to cool until firm. Cut into squares. Makes about 1 pound.

Crème de Menthe Turkish Delight

A simple way of making this delectable eastern sweet.
Preparation and cooking time: 1 hour and 24 hours

2 cups/500 g granulated sugar.
2 envelopes (1 tablespoon each)/30 ml unflavored gelatin.
1¼ cups/275 ml water. Green food color. Peppermint extract.
½ cup/50 g confectioners' sugar.
2 tablespoons/25 g cornstarch.

Dissolve granulated sugar and gelatin in the water in a large pan. Bring slowly to a boil and boil gently for 20 minutes. Remove from heat and add enough color to turn the mixture a delicate green. Add peppermint extract to taste. Pour into an 8-inch-square pan rinsed out in cold water. Set aside for 24 hours in a cool place. Mix together the confectioners' sugar and cornstarch. Dust your hands with this mixture and carefully pull the candy from the pan. Cut into strips, then into cubes; roll cubes in the sugar-cornstarch mixture.

Marrons glacé

A slight variation on the marrons glacé imported from France but delicious nonetheless.
Preparation and cooking time: 20 minutes and 3 days

1 cup/225 g granulated sugar. 2 cups/225 g confectioners' sugar.
⅔ cup/150 ml water.
2-2½ cups (15 oz.)/350 g canned chestnuts, drained (see note).
Vanilla.

Combine granulated sugar, confectioners' sugar and water and bring to a boil. Add the chestnuts and bring to a boil again. Let the chestnuts soak in the syrup overnight in a warm place. The next day bring the syrup to the boil again. Cover and set aside overnight. On the third day add a few drops of vanilla to the syrup and boil again. Transfer chestnuts to sterile canning jars, cover with syrup and seal.
Note: This recipe may be prepared with fresh chestnuts, too. Boil or roast about 1 pound fresh chestnuts, then shell and skin them before measuring.

Fruit Jellies

Sweets to make for children, with a taste of real fruit!
Preparation time: 15 minutes

1¼ cups/300 ml fruit juice. 1 cup/225 g sugar.
2 envelopes (1 tablespoon each)/30 ml unflavored gelatin.
Sugar for sprinkling.

Put the fruit juice in a pan with 1 cup sugar and the gelatin; dissolve carefully. Place over low heat. Rinse an 8-inch-square pan in cold water and pour in the heated liquid. Allow to set, then loosen jelly from the pan and cut into circles or fancy shapes.
Sprinkle with more sugar.

Barley Sugar

Store barley sugar in airtight tins or jars as this candy becomes sticky very quickly when exposed to air.
Preparation and cooking time: 20-25 minutes

2 cups/450 g sugar. 1¼ cups/300 ml water. Pinch cream of tartar.
6 drops lemon extract.

Lightly oil a work surface, preferably marble or enamel, although plastic laminate is satisfactory. Put the sugar, water and cream of tartar into a large heavy-based saucepan. Heat until sugar dissolves and then boil to 315° F or until the syrup has turned a pale amber color. Add the lemon extract. Pour the mixture onto the oiled surface and let cool a little. Fold the sides in to the middle and cut crosswise into strips with scissors. *Note:* To avoid recrystallization of the syrup when cooking make sure that the gas flame does not touch the side of the pan or, if you are using an electric range, that the burner is no larger than the base of the pan. Do not stir once syrup starts to boil.

PRALINE

Keep praline in an airtight container. It makes a delicious ingredient for ice creams or soufflés or as a decoration for cakes.
Preparation and cooking time: 30 minutes

½ cup/75 g unblanched almonds.
½ cup/75 g sugar (preferably superfine).

Put the two ingredients in a heavy-based pan and heat over low heat until the sugar melts. When mixture begins to turn a pale brown, stir with a metal spoon and continue cooking until a nut brown color. Turn out onto an oiled work surface and leave until set.
Crush to a powder as needed.

Russian Caramels

These are soft, chewy caramels and should be individually wrapped in squares of waxed paper or plastic wrap.
Preparation and cooking time: 30 minutes

1 cup/225 g granulated sugar. ½ cup/50 g light brown sugar.
½ cup/100 g butter. 2 tablespoons/50 g light corn syrup.
¼ cup/60 ml water.
¼ cup/60 ml light cream or evaporated milk. ½ teaspoon/2.5 ml vanilla.

Grease an 8-inch-square pan. Put sugars, 3 tablespoons butter, corn syrup and water into a large, heavy pan. Stir over low heat until sugars dissolve. Bring to a boil and continue cooking until candy thermometer reads 240° F or a bit of the mixture dropped into cold water indicates the soft-ball stage. Add cream and remaining butter. Stirring gently and continuously, cook until a drop in cold water indicates hard-ball stage or thermometer registers 255° F. Add vanilla and pour into prepared pan. Cut into squares when cold.
Makes a little over 1 pound.

Center Spread

Grapes in Caramel

This dish is a delicious treat in itself, but it may also be used as a decorative touch on cakes and other desserts. However, the grapes must be eaten on the same day that they are made.
Preparation and cooking time: 30 minutes

2 cups/450 g sugar. Pinch cream of tartar. 1¼ cups/275 ml water.
1 pound/450 g grapes, wiped dry. Small pleated-paper wrappers.

Brush a cookie sheet or work surface with oil. In a large heavy-based saucepan dissolve the sugar and cream of tartar in the water over low heat, stirring constantly. Increase the heat and boil until candy thermometer reads 300° F or a small amount dropped into water tests at hard-crack. Remove pan from heat. With a fork dip pairs of grapes into syrup. Place on cookie sheet and when set, transfer to paper wrappers. Other fruits which are suitable for coating with caramel are cherries, strawberries and orange segments.

■ Marzipan Petit Fours

This recipe may be used instead of a frosting for topping cakes.
It can also be modeled into fruits (as illustrated)
or into decorations for cakes.
Preparation time: 20-30 minutes

2 cups/225 g confectioners' sugar. 1 cup/225 g granulated sugar.
4 cups (1 lb.)/450 g ground almonds.
2 eggs, beaten. 1 teaspoon/5 ml vanilla.
Lemon juice. Food color.

Sift the confectioners' sugar into a bowl. Add the granulated sugar and almonds. Add the eggs and vanilla and just enough lemon juice to mix into a stiff dough. Knead lightly. Add food color and shape as desired.

◻ Coconut Kisses

Children can help to make these candies once the mixture is cooked.
Preparation and cooking time: 30 minutes

2½ cups/625 g sugar. ⅔ cup/150 ml water.
2 cups/150 g flaked coconut. Food color (optional).

Put sugar and water in a large, heavy saucepan and boil until candy thermometer reads 240° F or a bit of syrup dropped into cold water indicates the soft-ball stage. Remove from heat and stir in coconut and color, if desired. Form into "rocky" mounds on waxed paper or on a greased cookie sheet and leave until set.
Makes about 1¼ pounds.

◻ COCONUT ICE

Chocolate ice may be made by adding a tablespoon of cocoa powder to half the mixture.
Preparation and cooking time: 20 minutes

2 cups/500 g sugar. ⅔ cup/150 ml milk. 1⅓ cups/125 g flaked coconut.
Red food color.

Grease a small loaf pan. Put the sugar and milk together in a heavy saucepan and dissolve sugar over low heat. Bring to a boil and cook until candy thermometer reads 240° F or a bit dropped into cold water indicates the soft-ball stage. Remove from heat and stir in coconut. Pour half the mixture into the pan. Color the other half pink and pour on top of the white half. When set, turn out of pan and cut into slices.
Makes approximately 1¼ pounds.

■ Lemon Squash

This recipe may also be made with other citrus fruit.
The flavor is much more authentic than any
bottled drink bought in the supermarket.

Preparation and cooking time: 20 minutes

6 lemons. 8 cups/2 kg sugar. 7½ cups/1.5 liters water.
1 tablespoon/25 g citric acid.

Grate peel from all the lemons, then squeeze to extract juice. Set
juice aside. Boil the sugar, water and grated peel together for 10
minutes. Allow to cool and add the citric acid and the lemon juice.
Strain into bottles. Dilute to taste when serving.

ICED SUMMER PUNCH

To frost the rims of glasses for summer drinks, dip the rim of the glass first in beaten egg white and then in superfine sugar. Allow to dry for about 5 minutes.

Preparation time: 15 minutes

½ cup/100 g sugar. 1¼ cups/300 ml water. 1 cup/225 g dark rum. ⅓ cup/75 ml lime juice. Pinch grated nutmeg.

Dissolve the sugar in the water. Add the rum and lime juice and chill for about 1½ hours. Serve in frosted glasses with a slice of lemon or lime and sprinkle with nutmeg.

Mulled Punch

The recipe may be increased proportionately for parties but not more than six cinnamon sticks or six oranges should be used.

Preparation time: 30 minutes

¼ cup/50 g dark brown sugar. ⅔ cup/150 ml water. 1 bottle red wine. 2 oranges stuck with cloves. 2 cinnamon sticks. ⅔ cup/150 ml brandy.

In a large saucepan over low heat dissolve the sugar in the water. Add the wine, the oranges and the cinnamon sticks. Heat very slowly until almost boiling. Add the brandy. Strain into warm glasses and serve hot.

Apple Beer

To bruise gingerroot, place between the folds of a clean dish towel. Hammer with the end of a rolling pin.

Preparation time: 1 hour

2 pounds/1 kg (6 medium) cooking apples. 1 ounce/25 g gingerroot. 5 quarts/5 liters water. 2½ cups/650 g light corn syrup.

Wash apples and remove stems. Grate the whole fruit into a large plastic container. Add the bruised ginger and the water. Cover and set aside for a week, stirring daily. Stir in the corn syrup and strain through cheesecloth. Bottle in strong screw-top bottes. Keep for 2 weeks in a cool place before drinking.

Makes about 12 pints.

⊞ *Mocha Sauce*

This is one of the easiest and quickest sauces to make and is delicious poured over ice cream, stewed pears, cream puffs or éclairs.

Preparation and cooking time: 5 minutes

1 teaspoon/5 ml instant coffee powder. 2 teaspoons/10 ml hot water.
¼ cup/125 ml light corn syrup. ¼ cup/125 ml cocoa powder.

Dissolve the coffee powder in the hot water. Put coffee liquid and other ingredients into saucepan and stir over low heat until combined.

⊞ *Frothy Chocolate*

A delicious summer drink which may be served instead of a dessert.

Preparation time: 20 minutes

2 tablespoons/30 ml cocoa powder. ¼ cup/60 ml water.
⅓ cup/100 g light corn syrup. 1 egg, separated. 2½ cups/600 ml milk.
1 teaspoon/5 ml vanilla.

In a saucepan blend the cocoa powder, water and half the corn syrup and cook until smooth. Remove from heat and cool slightly. Add egg yolk, milk and vanilla. Strain and chill. Beat the egg white until stiff. Boil the remaining corn syrup for one minute. Pour slowly over beaten egg white, beating all the while. Float a spoonful of meringue on each glass of chocolate.

⊞ *Creme à la Vanille*

This is real custard and bears no comparison with a cornstarch-based "custard" sauce.

Preparation and cooking time: 20 minutes

2 egg yolks. 1¼ cups/275 ml milk. 2 tablespoons/30 ml sugar.
½ teaspoon/2.5 ml vanilla.

Beat yolks with a fork. Heat the milk and sugar together and pour onto the yolks. Stir and place in top of a double boiler over hot water. Stir until liquid will coat the back of a spoon. Add vanilla. Serve as a sauce.

⊞ *Foamy Orange Sauce*

A sweet-sharp sauce to serve warm over puddings. Try making it with pineapple juice instead of orange.

Preparation and cooking time: 20 minutes

2 eggs, separated. ⅔ cup/150 ml orange juice.
3 tablespoons/45 ml light corn syrup.
1 teaspoon/5 ml grated orange peel.
1 teaspoon/5 ml lemon juice.

Put the egg yolks, orange juice, corn syrup, peel and lemon juice in top of a double boiler over hot water and cook, stirring all the time, until the mixture thickens. Remove from heat. Beat the egg whites until stiff and fold into the yolk mixture.

Makes 4-6 servings.

◾ COFFEE FROSTING

This is a soft icing. The quantities given are sufficient to ice an 8-inch cake.
Preparation time: 10 minutes

1¾ cups/175 g confectioners' sugar. 1 tablespoon/25 g light corn syrup.
1 tablespoon/25 ml plus 2 teaspoons milk.
3 tablespoons/40 g margarine. 1 teaspoon/5 ml instant coffee powder,
dissolved in 2 teaspoons/10 ml hot water.

Sift the confectioners' sugar into a mixing bowl. Put the remaining ingredients into a small saucepan and stir over low heat until the margarine melts and the mixture is almost boiling. Pour into the sifted sugar and stir with a wooden spoon until smooth.
The icing can be used in several ways:
As a glaze -- pour over the cake as soon as the mixture is thick enough to coat the back of a spoon.
As a filling or frosting — allow the mixture to cool. Then beat briskly with a wooden spoon until it is the consistency of butter cream. Either spread between layers of a 2-layer cake as a filling or frost top and sides of cake and swirl frosting with a knife.
For decorating — when thick enough to hold its shape, put in pastry bag with star tip and pipe decorations on cake as desired.
Any leftover icing can be stored in the refrigerator and warmed in the top of a double boiler over hot water until it is once again of spreading consistency.

◾ Brandy Butter

Brandy butter is traditionally served with Christmas pudding or mince pies.
Preparation time: 10 minutes

½ cup/100 g butter. 1⅔ cups/300 g dark brown sugar. 1 egg yolk.
½ cup/100 ml brandy. Grated orange peel.

Beat the butter with half the sugar. Add the rest of the ingredients and beat well until creamy. This is a hard sauce and it will keep well under refrigeration for about three weeks.

Butterscotch Sauce

A rich, creamy sauce to serve with hot or cold puddings.
Preparation time: 10 minutes

⅓ cup/100 g light corn syrup. ½ cup/100 g light brown sugar.
2 tablespoons/25 g butter. 2 tablespoons/30 ml hot water.
¼ cup/60 ml evaporated milk. ½ teaspoon/2.5 ml vanilla.

Put corn syrup, sugar and butter in a saucepan and stir over low heat until sugar dissolves. Boil for three minutes. Remove from heat and add hot water carefully. Cool a little and add milk and vanilla. Serve either hot or cold. The sauce will be considerably thicker when cold.

Cakes & Cookies

DOUGHNUTS

Delicious with a cinnamon-sugar coating but still a treat even if you omit the cinnamon and use plain sugar.

Preparation and cooking time: 2-2½ hours

2 packages active dry yeast. 1¼ cups/300 ml warm milk.
4 cups/500 g flour. ¼ cup/50 g sugar. 1 teaspoon/5 ml salt.
¼ cup /50 g margarine. 1 egg. Deep fat or oil for frying.
Coating: ½ cup/100 g sugar. 1 teaspoon/5 ml cinnamon.

In a bowl dissolve the yeast in the warm milk (110° F). Add 1 cup of the flour and 1 teaspoon of the ¼ cup sugar. Let stand for 20 minutes until frothy. Mix the remaining flour, remaining sugar and the salt in another bowl and work in the margarine. Beat the egg and add it and the yeast mixture to the other ingredients. Knead well. Cover the bowl and put it in a warm place for about 1 hour so that the dough will rise. Knead again and then roll out dough to ½-inch thickness. Cut with a doughnut cutter and arrange doughnuts on a greased cookie sheet. Set aside for 20 minutes in a warm place to rise again. Fry rings slowly in deep, hot fat (375° F), about three at a time. Drain well on absorbent paper. Combine coating ingredients in a paper bag, drop doughnuts into the bag and shake well.

■ old fashioned Jumbles

The sugar, flour and cinnamon mixture used for rolling out the dough gives the finished cookies a crispy coating.

Preparation and cooking time: 30 minutes

½ cup/100 g margarine. ½ cup/100 g light brown sugar.
1¾ cups/200 g self-rising flour. 1 small egg, beaten.
Sprinkling:
2 tablespoons/25 g light brown sugar. ¼ cup/25 g flour.
1 teaspoon/5 ml cinnamon.
Decoration:
Halved almonds.

Cream the margarine and the ½ cup sugar together. Work in the flour and add enough beaten egg to make a stiff cookie dough. Divide into 32 pieces. Sift together the sprinkling ingredients and roll out the cookies in this mixture. With floured hands, roll each piece into a coil about ¼ inch thick. Bend the coils into fancy shapes — rounds, knots, S's, pressing each joining together firmly. Press an almond half into the top of each cookie. Then place the cookies on a greased cookie sheet and bake at 350° F for 15-20 minutes. Let cool on sheets until crisp, and store in an airtight container.

▦ COFFEE GINGERBREAD

A light-colored gingerbread with a subtle flavor that makes it ideal for teatime or coffee break.

Preparation and cooking time: 1 hour

1⅔ cups/175 g self-rising flour. 2 teaspoons/10 ml ground ginger. 2 teaspoons/10 ml instant coffee powder. ½ cup/100 ml hot water. ½ cup/100 g margarine. ⅓ cup/75 g light corn syrup. ¼ cup/50 g light brown sugar. 2 eggs, beaten.

Sift together flour and ginger into a bowl. Dissolve the coffee in the hot water. Melt margarine with corn syrup and sugar over low heat and pour into the dry ingredients. Mix in the eggs and the coffee mixture. Stir well. Pour into a greased and waxed-paper-lined 8-inch square pan and bake at 350° F for 40-45 minutes.

▦ *Canadian Gingerbread*

This is a rich, dark cake with the delectable stickiness that gingerbread should have.

Preparation and cooking time: 1 hour

2½ cups/275 g flour. 2 teaspoons/10 ml ground ginger. 2 teaspoons/10 ml cinnamon. 1 teaspoon/5 ml baking soda. ½ cup/100 g margarine. ½ cup/100 g light brown sugar, firmly packed. ½ cup/150 g molasses. ½ cup/150 g light corn syrup. 2 eggs, well beaten. ⅔ cup/150 ml hot water.

Sift together flour, spices and baking soda. Combine the margarine, sugar, molasses and corn syrup over low heat until the margarine melts. Pour into the dry ingredients. Add the eggs and the hot water. Mix well and pour into a greased and waxed-paper-lined 9-inch square baking dish. Bake at 350° F for about 45 minutes or until a toothpick inserted into the center comes out clean.

▦ JAPANESE CAKES

These delicious party cookies are something like macaroons in texture.

Preparation and cooking time: 2 hours

2 egg whites. ½ cup/100 g granulated sugar. ¾ cup/75 g ground almonds. Butter cream: 2 tablespoons/25 g butter. ½ cup/50 g confectioners' sugar. 2 teaspoons/10 ml cocoa powder. Icing: 2 squares (1 ounce each)/50 g semisweet chocolate.

Beat the egg whites until stiff, then beat in granulated sugar a little at a time. Fold in the ground almonds. Using a pastry bag with a round tube opening ½ inch in diameter, press the mixture into 2-inch lengths on a lightly oiled cookie sheet. Bake at 275° F for 1-1½ hours. Allow to cool. Cream together the ingredients for the butter cream, softening with a little hot water if necessary. Sandwich two cookies together with a filling of butter cream. Melt chocolate and dip ends of cookies into it as illustrated. Place on a wire rack to set.

▦ *Mincemeat Shortbread*

This is an excellent way to use up any mincemeat left over from Thanksgiving or the Christmas holiday season.

Preparation and cooking time: 1 hour

½ cup/100 g margarine or butter. ¼ cup/50 g sugar. 1½ cups/150 g flour. ¼ cup/60 ml mincemeat. Sugar for sprinkling.

Cream the margarine and sugar together and gradually work in the flour and mincemeat. Knead well and press mixture into a greased 8-inch round pan. Decorate edge with a fork and score into 8 or 12 wedges. Prick all over and bake at 325° F for 30-40 minutes until a pale golden brown. Cut along previously scored lines. Sprinkle with more sugar and let cool on a wire rack.

BATH BUNS

Rich, fruity buns with sugared tops to make for tea.
Preparation and cooking time: 2½ hours

4 cups/500 g flour. 2 packages active dry yeast.
⅔ cup/150 ml warm milk. ½ cup/75 g sugar. ⅔ cup/150 ml warm water.
1 teaspoon/5 ml salt. ¼ cup/50 g margarine. 3 eggs.
¾ cup/150 g raisins. ⅓ cup/50 g chopped candied fruit peel.
Crushed sugar cubes.

Sift 1 cup of the flour into a large bowl and make a well in the center.
Mix the yeast with half the warm milk (110° F) and 1 teaspoon of the
sugar and pour into the well. Add the rest of the milk and the water.
Stir together and leave in a warm place for 30 minutes until foamy.
Sift the rest of the flour and the salt into a bowl. Add the rest of the
sugar and work in the margarine. Pour in the yeast mixture. Beat 2 of
the eggs and add. Beat well, then add the raisins and fruit peel. Cover
the bowl and leave in a warm place until doubled in size. Knead well
and divide into 12 pieces. Shape each into a round and place on a
greased cookie sheet. Let rise again for 15 minutes.
Beat remaining egg and brush over buns. Sprinkle with crushed sugar.
Bake at 400° F for 15-20 minutes.

SELKIRK BANNOCKS

Split and toast bannocks for a highland tea – delicious with strawberry
preserves.
Preparation and cooking time: 2½ hours

2 cups/250 g flour. Pinch salt. ¼ cup/50 g lard. ⅔ cup/150 ml milk.
1 package active dry yeast. ¼ cup/50 g sugar. ½ cup/100 g raisins.
Glaze:
2 tablespoons/25 g sugar. 2 tablespoons/30 ml water.

Sift the flour and salt into a warm bowl. Melt the lard in a saucepan
and add the milk. Warm to 110° F, pour over the yeast and add 1
teaspoon of the ¼ cup sugar. Leave until frothy. Make a well in the
center of the flour and pour in the yeast liquid. Gradually work in the
flour and knead for 5 minutes. Cover the bowl and put it in a warm
place for 1 hour for dough to rise. Turn dough out onto a floured
working surface and knead in the raisins and remaining sugar. Shape
into one large round loaf or two smaller ones. Place on a greased
cookie sheet and let rise again for 15-20 minutes. Bake at 425° F
for 15 minutes and then reduce heat to 375° F for a further 25
minutes. Make a sugar glaze by dissolving the 2 tablespoons sugar in
the 2 tablespoons water. Brush over the bannocks as soon as they
are taken from the oven. Cool on a wire rack.

ANN'S COCONUT COOKIES

Oatmeal and coconut combined with corn syrup give these cookies a
pleasing, rough texture.
Preparation and cooking time: 1 hour

3 tablespoons/50 g light corn syrup. ⅔ cup/125 g margarine.
½ cup/100 g sugar. 1 cup/100 g flour. 1 cup/75 g rolled oats.
⅔ cup/50 g flaked coconut. 2 teaspoons/100 ml baking soda.
1 teaspoon hot water.

Heat corn syrup, margarine and sugar together until margarine melts
and sugar dissolves. Stir in the flour, rolled oats and coconut.
Dissolve the baking soda in the hot water. Add to the other
ingredients. Let mixture cool. Divide into 32 pieces and roll each
piece into a ball. Flatten and arrange cookies on greased cookie
sheets, allowing room for them to spread.
Bake at 325° F for 20 minutes.

◨ *Cinnamon Toast*

A very simple and quick dish to prepare. Try various whole wheat, whole grain and tea breads to make a more interesting base than plain white bread.

6 slices bread. ¼ cup/50 g butter
½ cup/100 g sugar. 2 teaspoons/10 ml cinnamon.

Place bread on a cookie sheet and toast one side under the broiler. Butter the untoasted side. Mix the sugar and cinnamon together and sprinkle onto the butter. Toast the sugared side under the broiler until just beginning to caramelize. Cut into finger-size strips.

◨ Treacle Scones

Scones are always best eaten on the day they are made. Serve these split and spread with butter.

Preparation and cooking time: 30 minutes

2 cups/225 g flour. 2 teaspoons/10 ml baking powder.
½ teaspoon/2.5 ml cinnamon. ¼ cup/50 g margarine.
2 tablespoons/25 g sugar.
2 tablespoons/25 g dark molasses. ⅔ cup/150 ml milk.

Sift flour, baking powder and cinnamon into a bowl. Work in the margarine and add the sugar. Stir in the molasses and enough milk to make a soft dough. Roll out to ½-inch thickness. Cut into rounds and put on a greased cookie sheet. Bake at 425° F for 10-15 minutes.

Golden Oatcakes

The corn syrup produces a softer, chewier cookie with a butterscotch flavor.
Preparation and cooking time: 40 minutes

*2 cups/150 g rolled oats. ½ cup/100 g light brown sugar, firmly packed.
6 tablespoons/75 g margarine. ¼ cup/50 g light corn syrup.*

Mix rolled oats and sugar together in a bowl. Combine margarine and corn syrup in a saucepan, heat until margarine melts and add the dry ingredients. Stir together and press into a greased 8-inch square pan.
Bake at 350° F for 20 minutes.

Feather Iced Cakes

Try various color combinations – chocolate and white look very effective on a party table.

Preparation and cooking time: 45 minutes

¼ cup/50 g margarine. ¼ cup/50 g granulated sugar
1 egg, beaten. ½ cup/50 g self-rising flour.
Icing:
1 cup/100 g confectioners' sugar. 1 tablespoon/15 ml warm water.
Food color.

Cream the margarine and granulated sugar until pale-colored and creamy. Add beaten egg gradually, beating all the time. Fold in the flour. Divide the mixture into 12 pleated-paper cups set in shallow muffin tins. Bake for 15 -20 minutes at 325° F. Let cool. For the icing mix confectioners' sugar and warm water. Color one-third of the icing. Spread the white icing on the cakes and pipe lines of the contrasting color across. Draw a knife point across the color lines to make "feathers" (see illustration). Set aside to harden.

SPICED RASPBERRY BUNS

Raspberry buns were favorites at Victorian children's parties.

Preparation and cooking time: 40 minutes

4 cups/500 g flour. 1 tablespoon/15 ml baking powder. Pinch salt.
½ teaspoon/2.5 ml cinnamon. ¼ teaspoon/1.2 ml ground cloves.
¼ teaspoon/1.2 ml nutmeg. ¾ cup/150 g margarine. ¾ cup/150 g sugar.
2 eggs, beaten. ⅔ cup/150 ml milk. Raspberry jam.

Sift together the flour, baking powder, salt and spices. Cut in the margarine and stir in the sugar. Add the eggs. Add just enough milk to bind the mixture together into a stiff dough. Divide into 24 pieces and roll each into a ball. Place balls on a greased cookie sheet. Make a well in each with a fingertip and spoon a little jam into the well. Brush the tops with milk and sprinkle with sugar. Bake at 425° F for 10-15 minutes. After baking, add a little more jam to each bun.

Swedish Tea Ring

A festive ring cake with a rich, almond-flavored filling.

Preparation and cooking time: 2 hours

⅔ cup/150 ml milk. ½ teaspoon/2.5 ml active dry yeast.
2 tablespoons/25 g granulated sugar. 2 tablespoons/25 g margarine.
2 cups/250 g flour. 1 egg, beaten. ¼ cup/50 g margarine, softened.
½ cup/50 g ground almonds.
¼ cup/50 g dark brown sugar, firmly packed.
Topping:
1 cup/100 g confectioners' sugar.
Warm water. ¼ cup/25 g slivered almonds.

Heat milk to approximately 110° F and add yeast and granulated sugar. Cut the 2 tablespoons margarine into the flour. Add yeast mixture and egg. Beat well. Cover bowl and set aside for dough to rise for 1 hour. Knead and roll out to an oblong approximately 12 inches by 9 inches. Spread with ¼ cup softened margarine and sprinkle with ground almonds and dark brown sugar. Roll up jelly-roll fashion, then form a ring and seal ends together with water. Take kitchen shears and, at intervals of about one inch, snip all around outer edge of ring, cutting not quite through to the center. Transfer to a greased cookie sheet and set aside to rise for 20 minutes in a warm place. Bake at 425° F for 15 minutes. Reduce heat to 350° F and continue baking for 15 minutes longer. To make the topping, blend confectioners' sugar with a little warm water. Spread over ring and decorate with slivered almonds.

Easter Cookies

In small plastic boxes, these sugar-topped cookies make lovely Easter gifts.

Preparation and cooking time: 40 minutes

½ cup/100 g sugar. 6 tablespoons/75 g margarine. 1 egg yolk.
1⅓ cups/150 g self-rising flour. ½ teaspoon/2.5 ml cinnamon.
¼ teaspoon/1.2 ml ground cloves. ¼ teaspoon/1.2 ml nutmeg.
1 tablespoon/10 g mixed candied fruit peel. ¼ cup/50 g currants.
1 tablespoon/15 ml milk. Sugar for sprinkling.

Cream the sugar and margarine together. Beat in the egg yolk and gradually work in the flour, spices and then the fruit peel and the currants, adding just enough milk to make a stiff dough. Roll out to ¼-inch thickness and cut into 2-inch rounds. Place on a greased cookie sheet. Prick with a fork and bake for 20 minutes at 350° F. When baked, sprinkle lightly with sugar.

VANILLA SLICE

This is one of the great classic cakes, filled with pastry cream.

Preparation and cooking time: 1½ hours

8 ounces/250 g frozen puff pastry.
2 egg yolks. ¼ cup/50 g granulated sugar. 1 tablespoon/15 ml cornstarch.
1 tablespoon/15 ml flour. 1¼ cups/275 ml milk. 1 egg white.
Few drops vanilla. Strawberry or raspberry jam. Confectioners' sugar.

Defrost and roll out pastry thinly. Cut into three equal oblongs. Bake on a greased cookie sheet in a hot oven (425° F) for 15-25 minutes or until golden. Transfer to a wire rack to cool. Beat egg yolks and granulated sugar together. Sift the cornstarch and the flour into the egg-sugar mixture and add half the milk. Bring the rest of the milk to a boil and pour onto the egg-sugar mixture. Blend well and return to the pan, stirring over low heat until the mixture thickens. Remove from heat and cool. Beat the egg white until stiff and fold into the cream. Add vanilla. Spread one pastry oblong with half the cream and some jam. Top with the second layer, then the rest of the cream and more jam. Top with the third layer and sprinkle the top liberally with confectioners' sugar.

■ Apricot Tea Bread

A delicious fruit-and-nut tea bread, which can be eaten as is or sliced thin and buttered.

Preparation and cooking time: 2¼ hours

1 cup/100 g dried apricots. 1¾ cups/225 g self-rising flour.
½ cup/50 g chopped almonds. ¼ cup/50 g light brown sugar.
¼ cup/50 g margarine. ⅓ cup/100 g light corn syrup.
1 egg, beaten. ⅓ cup milk.

Pour boiling water onto the apricots and let soak for about 1 hour — until they are plump and soft but not soggy. Drain and cut into small pieces. Put flour into a bowl. Stir in the apricots, almonds and sugar. Over low heat, melt margarine with corn syrup. Remove from heat and add the beaten egg and milk. Mix into the dry ingredients. Pour into a greased 8½ x 4½-inch loaf pan. Bake at 350° F for 1 hour.

❑ Nutty Meringues

The mixture can also be piped into rounds on greased paper and the rounds filled with fresh fruit after baking.

Preparation and cooking time: 2½ hours

1 cup/100 g whole filberts. 2 egg whites.
½ cup/100 g sugar. 5 drops vanilla.

Set aside about 16 whole nuts for decoration. Crush the rest finely with a rolling pin. Beat the egg whites until they are stiff and form soft peaks. Add half the sugar and continue beating until whites stand in stiff peaks. Fold in the rest of the sugar, the crushed nuts and the vanilla. Either pipe the meringue mixture or drop teaspoonfuls onto a greased cookie sheet. Put a whole nut on the top of each and bake at 250° F for 2-3 hours until crisp all the way through.

❑ Banana Nut Bread

The flavors of bananas and walnuts blend in this moist tea bread.

Preparation and cooking time: 1¼ hours

1¾ cups/225 g self-rising flour. ¼ cup/50 g margarine.
¼ cup/50 g sugar. ½ cup/50 g chopped walnuts. 2 bananas.
1 egg. ¼ cup/75 g light corn syrup. Milk.

Grease an 8½ x 4½-inch loaf pan. Put flour in a bowl and blend in the margarine. Add the sugar and walnuts. In a second bowl, mash the bananas. Beat the egg into the banana pulp and add the corn syrup. Pour into dry ingredients and mix well, adding just enough milk to make mixture a soft consistency. Pour into pan and bake at 350° F for about 1 hour. Store for at least 24 hours before slicing and serving.

■ *Danish Pastries*

They may look difficult but it is possible to prepare these
professional-looking Danish pastries at home.

Preparation and cooking time: 1½ hours

*⅔ cup/150 ml milk. 2 packages active dry yeast. ¼ cup/50 g sugar.
4 cups/450 g flour. 1¼ cups/250 g butter. 2 eggs, beaten.*

Heat milk to approximately 110° F and pour onto the yeast. Add 1
teaspoon of the sugar and leave for 20 minutes until the yeast proofs
and mixture is foamy. Put the flour in a bowl, add the remaining sugar
and blend in ¼ cup of the butter. Add the yeast mixture and the eggs.
Shape the remaining butter into a block. Roll out dough into an oblong
and place butter block in center. Fold upper third of dough to center,
covering butter. Fold bottom third of dough completely over the
double layer, making a three-layered envelope. Press edges with
rolling pin to seal. Give dough a quarter-turn. Once again, roll out the
dough into an oblong and then fold and seal the edges as before.
Repeat this process two more times. Put dough into a plastic bag,
place in refrigerator and chill for 15-20 minutes before using. If dough
becomes difficult to handle at any time during this process, allow it to
rest in the plastic bag in the refrigerator for 20 minutes before
attempting to roll it out again. Dough may be stored in the refrigerator
for 24 hours before using. Or it can be prepared, wrapped in plastic
wrap and foil and frozen for later use. When ready to use, roll out thin,
prepare filling and shape as illustrated.

Fillings:
*For windmills: 4 ounces/100 g marzipan, candied cherries.
For triangles: 1 chopped eating apple,
2 tablespoons/30 ml apricot jam
For whirls: ¼ cup/50 g butter, ¼ cup/50 g sugar,
2 teaspoons/10 ml cinnamon, ¼ cup/50 g currants*
Put on greased baking sheets to rise and leave pastries in warm place
for 20 minutes. Bake at 425° F for 15 minutes.

Walnut Layer Cake
with American Frosting

A layer cake to make for special occasions. Soft American frosting is used for the topping.
Preparation and cooking time: 1 hour

Cake:
1 cup/200 g margarine. ½ cup/100 g light brown sugar.
⅓ cup/100 g light corn syrup. 4 eggs. 1¾ cups/200 g self-rising flour.
1 cup/100 g chopped walnuts.
Filling:
2 cups/200 g confectioners' sugar. ½ cup/100 g butter.
½ cup/50 g chopped walnuts.
Frosting:
1 cup/225 g granulated sugar. ¼ cup/60 ml water. 1 egg white.
Walnut halves for decoration.

Cream the margarine, brown sugar and corn syrup together until soft and light-colored. Beat the eggs and add them gradually to the creamed ingredients. Fold in the flour and the cup of chopped walnuts. Divide the mixture among three 8-inch greased and floured pans. (Springform pans or those with removable bottoms are preferred.) Bake at 370° F for 25-30 minutes. Cool on wire racks. To make the filling, sift confectioners' sugar, then cream it together with the butter until mixture is soft. Stir in the ½ cup of chopped nuts. Sandwich the layers together with this butter cream. Prepare the frosting by heating granulated sugar and water together until sugar dissolves and mixture reaches the boiling point. Continue to boil without stirring until candy thermometer reads 240° F or a drop of syrup in water tests at the soft-ball stage. Beat the egg white until stiff. Pour the sugar syrup slowly over the egg white, beating all the while, until mixture thickens. Spread quickly over the cake and decorate with walnut halves.

Lardy Cake

Lardy cake is really a tea bread and is best eaten warm, almost straight from the oven.
Preparation and cooking time: 2½ hours

⅔ cup/150 ml milk. 1 package active dry yeast.
2 tablespoons/25 g granulated sugar. 2 tablespoons/25 g margarine.
2 cups/250 g flour. 6 tablespoons/75 g lard.
½ cup/100 g light brown sugar. 1 teaspoon/5 ml cinnamon.
½ teapoon/2.5 ml ground cloves. ½ teaspoon/2.5 ml nutmeg.
1 cup/100 g dried fruit. Milk.

Heat milk to approximately 110° F and pour onto the yeast. Add 1 teaspoon of the granulated sugar. Set aside until the yeast proofs and the mixture is foamy. Blend the margarine into the flour and add the remaining granulated sugar. Add the yeast mixture and knead for 5 minutes. Cover bowl and put in a warm place for 1 hour for dough to rise. Turn out onto floured work surface and knead again. Roll out into an oblong about 12 inches by 6 inches. Spread one-third of the lard on the upper two-thirds of the oblong. Combine the brown sugar and the spices and sprinkle one-third of this mixture and then one-third of the fruit over the same area of the dough as was spread with the lard. Fold up the dough by bringing the bottom third up to cover the center portion and then fold the upper third over that. Seal the edges with a light touch of the rolling pin. Then repeat the process of rolling the dough into an oblong, spreading the lard and sprinkling with the sugar and spice mixture and then the fruit two more times until all the ingredients have been used. Roll out the dough to ½-inch thickness and put in a greased baking pan. Score the top in a crisscross pattern. Set aside to rise until doubled in size. Brush with a little milk and bake at 400° F for 30 minutes.
Serve warm.

MARSHMALLOW CRISPIES

Quick and easy cookies — so simple that even children can make them.
Preparation and cooking time: 10 minutes

¼ cup/50 g sugar. ¼ cup/50 g margarine. ½ cup/150 g light corn syrup.
1½ cups/50 g miniature marshmallows (or about 8 large marshmallows). 5 cups/100 g crisp rice cereal.

Put the sugar, margarine and corn syrup in a saucepan and heat gently until the sugar dissolves. Bring to a boil and stir in the marshmallows. Add the cereal and stir it into the mixture until evenly coated. Spoon into paper baking cups. Makes about 16.

Bakewell Tart

Bakewell tarts were being made in Derbyshire more than a hundred years ago.
Preparation and cooking time: 45 minutes

Pastry:
6 tablespoons/75 g margarine. 1½ cups/150 g all-purpose flour.
Filling:
⅓ cup/100 g raspberry jam. 6 tablespoons/75 g margarine.
⅓ cup/75 g sugar. 1 egg. 1 teaspoon/5 ml almond extract.
½ cup/50 g self-rising flour. ¼ cup/25 g ground almonds.

Prepare a pie dough by cutting 6 tablespoons of margarine into the all-purpose flour and binding together with a little cold water. Roll out and line an 8-inch pie pan. Spread with jam. Prepare the rest of the filling by creaming 6 tablespoons margarine and the sugar and then beating in the egg and almond extract. Stir in the self-rising flour and ground almonds. Spread over the jam and bake at 375° F for 20 minutes.

◧ *Madeleines*

Pretty cakes for a party, jam-covered and sprinkled with coconut.
Preparation and cooking time: 45 minutes

½ cup/100 g margarine. ½ cup/100 g sugar. 2 eggs, beaten.
1 cup/100 g self-rising flour. ⅓ cup/100 g red jam.
⅔ cup/50 g flaked coconut. Candied cherries.
Candied fruit peel or angelica.

Cream margarine and sugar together until light-colored and fluffy. Add beaten eggs and mix thoroughly. Sift the flour and fold in. Fill 12 greased dariole molds (see note) about two-thirds full. Bake at 325° F for 10-15 minutes. Turn out and let cool. Strain the jam, if necessary, and slightly warm it in a saucepan. Brush the sides and tops of the cakes with jam. Dip and roll in coconut. Decorate with cherries and candied fruit peel.

Note: The dariole mold traditionally used in this recipe measures approximately 2 inches high. It is 1½ inches wide at the top and 1 inch wide at the bottom. Any ovenproof container about the same size could be substituted — perhaps some custard cups or even sturdy earthenware demitasse cups.

▣ ECCLES CAKES

One of the great British regional cakes, rich with fruit and sugar.
Preparation and cooking time: 45 minutes

Pastry:
2 cups/225 g flour. ¾ cup/150 g margarine.
Filling:
2 tablespoons/25 g margarine. 2 tablespoons/25 g dark brown sugar.
½ cup/100 g currants. Granulated sugar for sprinkling.

Make a flaky pastry by cutting a quarter of the ¾ cup margarine into the flour. Add about 8 tablespoons cold water and mix into a soft dough. Roll out into an oblong 12 inches by 8 inches and put another quarter of the margarine on the upper two-thirds of the pastry. Fold the dough into thirds by bringing the bottom third up to cover the center portion and then the top third over that. Repeat this rolling and folding process two more times, using the remaining two quarters of margarine. Then repeat the rolling and folding without adding any margarine. Put the pastry in a cool place. Melt the 2 tablespoons margarine for the filling. Add the brown sugar and the currants. Roll the pastry out into a large oblong and cut into twelve oblongs. Spoon some filling into the center of each. Wet the edges of each piece of pastry and gather into a round pouch enclosing the filling. Seal the edges together. Turn over and flatten with a rolling pin. Cut through the top of each cake twice. Brush with water and sprinkle with granulated sugar. Bake on greased cookie sheets at 400° F for 15-20 minutes.

▣ Refrigerator Cookies

Various flavorings can be added to this basic cookie mixture. It can be kept in the refrigerator for at least a week and cookies baked as they are needed.
Preparation and cooking time: 30 minutes

1 cup/225 g sugar. ½ cup/100 g margarine. 1 egg.
1 teaspoon/5 ml vanilla. 3 cups/300 g flour.
2 teaspoons/10 ml baking powder.

Cream sugar and margarine together until soft. Beat in the egg and vanilla. Sift flour and baking powder together and gradually work into other ingredients. Mix well and shape into a roll. Refrigerate for 24 hours. Cut into thin slices and bake on a greased cookie sheet at 375° F for 7-10 minutes

◧ Genoese Fancies

Genoese sponge is a little more difficult to make than an ordinary sponge cake but it has better keeping qualities and a superior texture.

Preparation and cooking time: 1 hour

5 eggs. ⅔ cup/125 g sugar. 1¼ cups/125 g flour. ⅓ cup/60 g butter.

Beat the eggs and sugar together in the top of a double boiler over hot water until pale-colored and thick. Sift the flour and fold it in. Melt butter and drizzle it into the mixture, folding until all ingredients are well blended. Pour into two greased and lined 8-inch square pans. Bake at 350° F for 25 minutes. Cool on wire rack, cut into shapes and decorate with your favorite frosting or as illustrated.

◧ CHOCOLATE NESTS

Ideal cakes to make for a children's Easter party or a birthday party.

Preparation and cooking time: 20 minutes

¾ cup/150 g margarine. ½ cup/100 g dark brown sugar.
⅓ cup/100 g light corn syrup. ¾ cup/50 g cocoa powder.
1½ cups/150 g crushed shredded wheat (6 large biscuits).
Candy eggs.

Melt margarine with brown sugar and corn syrup in a pan. Stir in the cocoa powder. Pour chocolate mixture onto shredded wheat and mix well. Shape into 12 nests and allow to set on a greased cookie sheet. Fill with candy eggs.

◧ Simnel Cake

In Britain this cake is traditionally made for Mothering Sunday (Mother's Day) or Easter. If made for Easter, it should be decorated with eleven marzipan balls, which represent the disciples without Judas.

Preparation and cooking time: 3½ hours

1 cup/250 g margarine. 1 cup/250 g light brown sugar. 4 eggs.
Grated peel of 1 lemon. ½ cup/50 g ground almonds.
2 cups/250 g flour. ¼ teaspoon/1.2 ml cinnamon.
¼ teaspoon/1.2 ml nutmeg. 1 cup/250 g dark raisins.
1 cup/250 g seedless white raisins. 1 cup/250 g currants.
½ cup/100 g mixed candied fruit peel. 1½ pounds/750 g marzipan.

Grease and line with waxed paper a deep 8-inch round springform or charlotte russe mold. Preheat oven to 275° F. Cream together the margarine and brown sugar. Beat the eggs, add them to the creamed ingredients and beat well. Add the grated lemon peel and the ground almonds. Sift together the flour and spices and fold in. Add the raisins, currants and fruit peel. Divide the batter in half and put half in cake pan. Roll out one-third of the marzipan to an 8-inch circle and put on top of the batter already in the pan. Spread the remaining half of the batter over the marzipan. Bake for 3-3½ hours. Decorate the top with the remaining marzipan.

Hearts and Flowers Cake

Various colorings and fillings could be added to both the cake and the
butter cream filling.

Preparation and cooking time: 1 hour

Cake:
1 cup/250 g margarine. 1 cup/250 g granulated sugar. 4 eggs.
1¾ cups/250 g self-rising flour.
Filling:
½ cup/100 g margarine. 2 cups/200 g confectioners' sugar.
Decoration:
Crystallized flowers. Angelica.

Cream 1 cup margarine and the granulated sugar until light and fluffy.
Beat in the eggs gradually. Sift the flour and fold in. Divide mixture
and transfer to two greased and waxed-paper-lined 8½-inch
heart-shaped pans. Bake at 350° F for 25-35 minutes. Cream
½ cup margarine and the confectioners' sugar together to
make the butter cream, adding a little hot water if necessary. Spread
between layers and pipe on top of cake. Decorate with crystallized
flowers and angelica.

Preserves

Banana Jam

A quick-to-make preserve that has a delicious and unusual flavor. It is particularly good with plain scones.

Preparation and cooking time: 1 hour

1 pound/500 g bananas. 3¾ cups/800 ml canned orange juice. Juice of 1 lemon. 1½ cups/350 g dark brown sugar.

Cut up bananas and put all ingredients together in a pan. Bring to a boil and then cook slowly until bananas soften and mixture becomes thick and turns a rich red color. Stir frequently to prevent scorching. Transfer to hot sterilized jars and seal. When cool, refrigerate. Use within a few weeks.

Gooseberry and Elderflower Jelly

The elderflowers add a very delicate flavor to the gooseberries and can be used in the same way in any cooked gooseberry recipe.

Preparation and cooking time: 2 hours

4 pounds/2 kg gooseberries. 1¼ quarts/1.5 liters water. 6 heads elderflowers. Sugar.

Wash the gooseberries but do not remove stem and blossom ends. Put in a pan and add 1 quart/1 liter of the water and the elderflower heads tied in cheesecloth. Simmer until fruit is tender. Mash fruit. Strain through a jelly bag or a double layer of cheesecloth. Drain for 15 minutes. Reserve liquid. Transfer the pulp from the jelly bag to the pan, add the remaining water and simmer again for 30 minutes. Strain and drain again. Discard pulp. Combine the two liquids. Measure and add 1⅔ cups sugar for each cup of juice. Bring to the boiling point,
stir to dissolve the sugar, and boil until jellying point is reached, 220°-222°F on a jelly thermometer. Or dip a large spoon into the boiling mixture, let juice cool a bit, tilt the spoon and let juice drop back into the pan. If, as you tilt the spoon, the juice first separates into two distinct drops but then runs together and slides off the spoon in a sheet, the jellying point has been reached. Then pour into sterilized jelly glasses and seal.

◼ Mustard Pickle

Mustard pickle — or piccalilli as it is also called — is a good way of using up a surplus of late summer vegetables.

Preparation and cooking time: 1 hour and 24 hours

3 pounds/1.5 kg vegetable mixture (cucumbers, green beans,
green tomatoes, small onions, cauliflower, summer squash).
1 cup/225 g salt. 2½ quarts/2 liters water. ¼ cup/25 g flour.
2 teaspoons/10 ml turmeric. 1 teaspoon/5 ml dry mustard..
1 quart/750 ml white vinegar. ⅔ cup/125 g sugar.
1 teaspoon/5 ml ground ginger.

Wash and cut up the vegetables and place them in a large bowl. Dissolve the salt in the water and pour over vegetables. Let stand for 24 hours. Rinse and drain. Blend the flour, turmeric and mustard with enough vinegar to make a thin paste. Set aside. Simmer the vegetables for 20 minutes in the remaining vinegar combined with the sugar and ginger. Remove the vegetables with a slotted spoon and transfer to hot sterilized jars. Add the blended flour mixture to the hot liquid and bring to a boil. Boil for 1 minute and pour over the vegetables, filling the jars to within ¼ inch of the top. Seal and place in a boiling water bath for 15 minutes. Label when cool.

◻ Bread & Butter Relish

A mild-flavored relish for cold meats that is also quite delicious spread on buttered bread or used as a sandwich filling.

Preparation and cooking time: 1 hour and 3 hours

2 cucumbers. 1 pound/500 g (about 6 medium) onions.
1 large green pepper. ¼ cup/50 g salt.
Syrup: 2 cups/500 g sugar. 1 teaspoon/5 ml mustard seed.
½ teaspoon/2.5 ml turmeric. ½ teaspoon/2.5 ml celery seed.
1¼ cups/300 ml cider vinegar. ⅔ cup/150 ml water.

Wash cucumbers and slice thin. Peel and slice onions thin. Remove seeds from pepper and slice thin. Mix vegetables and salt together in a bowl and let stand for 3 hours. Rinse and drain well. Combine all the syrup ingredients together in a large saucepan. Bring to a boil and boil for 6 minutes. Add the drained vegetables and bring slowly to the boiling point. Remove pan from heat and pour relish into hot sterilized pint-size jars. Seal and place in a boiling water bath for 10 minutes. Label when cool.

◻ Ripe Tomato Chutney

Crisp eating apples can be used instead of cooking apples if you happen to have a late summer surplus, but cooking apples give a better flavor.

Preparation and cooking time: 1½ hours

1⅓ cups/250 g chopped onions. 1¼ cups/300 ml vinegar.
2 pounds/1 kg (about 8 medium) ripe tomatoes, peeled and sliced.
2 cups/250 g peeled, cored, chopped apples.
1 cup/250 g seedless white raisins.
1 teaspoon/5 ml pickling spices, tied in cheesecloth.
2 teaspoons/10 ml dry mustard. ½ teaspoon/2.5 ml ground ginger.
½ teaspoon/2.5 ml salt. ½ teaspoon/2.5 ml pepper. 2 cups/500 g sugar

Simmer the onions in 4 tablespoons/60 ml of the vinegar until soft. Add the tomatoes, apples, raisins, bag of pickling spices, mustard, ginger, salt and pepper. Simmer gently until the fruits are soft. Add the remaining vinegar and the sugar. Stir to dissolve the sugar and boil mixture gently until it is thick. Remove bag of pickling spices, and pour chutney into hot sterilized pint-size jars. Seal and place in a boiling water bath for 10 minutes. Label when cool.

◻ Apple & Raisin Chutney

A very simple pickle to make. It needs no cooking at all.

Preparation time: 1 hour

3 pounds/1½ kg (about 9 medium) cooking apples.
1 pound/500 g (about 6) onions. ⅓ cup/50 g mustard seed.
2 cups/500 g seedless white raisins. 1 rounded tablespoon/15 ml salt.
2 cups/500 g sugar. 2½ cups/600 ml white vinegar.
½ teaspoon/2.5 ml cayenne pepper. 2 teaspoons/10 ml ground ginger.

Peel, core and quarter the apples. Peel and quarter the onions. Chop the apples and onion coarsely and put in a large mixing bowl. Add the rest of the ingredients and stir thoroughly. Cover and leave in a cool place for one week, stirring each day. Put in jars and cover. Refrigerate. Use within 2 weeks.

■ *Plum Chutney*

A rich brown chutney with a delicious spicy flavor. It is equally
delicious when made with Damson plums.

Preparation and cooking time: 2 hours

1 teaspoon/5 ml ground cloves. 1 teaspoon/5 ml ground ginger.
1 teaspoon/5 ml ground allspice. 2 tablespoons/25 g salt.
2½ cups/600 ml vinegar. 1 cup/250 g light brown sugar.
7 cups/1 kg pitted, quartered red plums.
2 cups/250 g peeled, cored, chopped apples. ½ cup/100 g raisins.
1⅓ cups/250 g chopped onions. ¾ cup/100 g sliced carrots.

Blend the spices and salt with a little of the vinegar. Put the remaining
vinegar and the sugar in a large pan and bring slowly to the boil. Add the
fruits and vegetables and stir in the spice mixture. Simmer until thick. Put
in hot sterilized jars, cover and seal. When cool, refrigerate. Use within
a few weeks.

◻ Orchard Marmalade

This is a very useful recipe to make when all your orange marmalade has been eaten and Seville oranges — the best variety for marmalade — are not available for making more. Orchard marmalade has a mild flavor.

Preparation and cooking time: 3 hours

1 orange. 1 grapefruit. 1 lemon. 1 large cooking apple. 1 pear.
2 quarts/1.5 liters water. 6 cups/1.5 kg sugar.

Squeeze citrus fruit to extract juice; remove seeds. Set aside. Remove and chop the peels. Peel, quarter and core the apple and pear; reserve cores and chop both fruits. Tie citrus seeds and apple and pear cores in a cheesecloth bag. Put all chopped fruit, juice, cheesecloth bag and water in a large canning kettle. Simmer gently for about 2 hours or until the volume is reduced by one-third. Remove cheesecloth bag and squeeze dry over kettle. Add the sugar, stir until it dissolves and then bring mixture to a rolling boil. Boil for 15 minutes and test for jellying point: Put a little of mixture on a saucer. When cool, it should wrinkle when pushed with the finger. When jellying point is reached, pour the marmalade into hot sterilized jars and seal with paraffin. Cover and label when cool.

◻ Tangerine Marmalade

Make this marmalade around Christmas time, when tangerines are at their best.

Preparation and cooking time: 2 hours

1 pound/500 g (about 5) tangerines. 1 teaspoon/5 ml lemon juice.
1 quart/900 ml water. 3 cups/750 g sugar.

Wash and peel the tangerines; cut peel into strips. Cut each tangerine in half; squeeze to extract juice; remove seeds and tie them in a cheesecloth bag. Put peel, tangerine juice, lemon juice, water and seeds in a large pan. Cook slowly until volume is reduced by one-third. Add sugar and bring to a boil, stirring all the time, until sugar dissolves. Boil until jellying point is reached, 220°-222° F on a jelly thermometer. Or dip a large spoon into the boiling mixture, let juice cool a bit, tilt the spoon and let juice drop back into the pan. If, as you tilt the spoon, the juice first separates into two distinct drops but then runs together and slides off the spoon in a sheet, the jellying point has been reached. Then pour into hot sterilized jars, cover and label. When cool, refrigerate. Use within a few weeks.

◼ Orange Jelly Marmalade

This recipe is economical because the yield from the weight of fruit is high.

Preparation and cooking time: 3½ hours

2 pounds/1 kg (about 5) Seville or navel oranges.
2¾ quarts/2.5 liters water. Juice of 2 lemons. 6 cups/1.5 kg sugar.

Wash the oranges and peel them. Cut peel into thin strips and put in a cheesecloth bag. Cut the peeled fruit into small pieces and put into a canning kettle or a large pot along with the water, lemon juice and the cheesecloth bag of peel. Bring to a boil and simmer for about 2 hours or until volume is reduced by one-third. Strain through a jelly bag or several layers of cheesecloth and allow to drip. Do not squeeze bag or the jelly will be cloudy. Return strained juice to kettle and add sugar. Stir until sugar dissolves and then add strips of peel from the cheesecloth bag.

Boil until the jellying point is reached, 220°-222° F on a jelly thermometer. Or dip a large spoon into the boiling mixture, let juice cool a bit, tilt the spoon and let juice drop back into the kettle. If, as you tilt the spoon, the juice first separates into two distinct drops but then runs together and slides off the spoon in a sheet, the jellying point has been reached. Then skim and let cool before pouring into warm sterilized jars. The cooling prevents the peel from rising to the top. Seal and label. Refrigerate. Use within a few weeks.

■ Whiskey Marmalade

The small amount of whiskey produces a subtle and delicious flavor.
Preparation and cooking time: 3½ hours

2 pounds/1 kg (about 5) Seville or navel oranges. Juice of 2 lemons.
2½ quarts/2.5 liters water. 8 cups/2 kg sugar.
⅔ cup/150 ml Scotch whiskey.

Wash and peel the oranges; finely chop peel. Cut each orange in half; squeeze to extract juice; remove seeds and tie them in a cheesecloth bag. Put peel, orange juice, lemon juice, water and seeds in a large pot or canning kettle. Bring to a boil and simmer for about 2 hours or until volume is reduced by one-third. Remove cheesecloth and, when cool, squeeze the jelly-like substance in it back into the kettle. Add sugar and heat until it dissolves. Add whiskey. Bring to a boil and boil rapidly until jellying point is reached, 220°-222° F on a jelly thermometer. Or dip a large spoon into the boiling mixture, let juice cool a bit, tilt the spoon and let juice drop back into the pot. If, as you tilt the spoon, the juice first separates into two distinct drops but then runs together and slides off the spoon in a sheet, jellying point has been reached. Then pour into hot sterilized jars and seal. When cool, refrigerate. Use within a few weeks.

■  Rhubarb Ginger Jam

A very good preserve to serve with steamed puddings — or simply spoon over ice cream.

Preparation and cooking time: 45 minutes and 24 hours

2 pounds/1 kg rhubarb. 4 cups/1 kg sugar. Juice of 2 lemons.
1 ounce/25 g gingerroot.
4 ounces (¾ cup)/100 g chopped crystallized ginger.

Wash and trim rhubarb. Cut into 1-inch pieces and layer in a china or glass bowl with the sugar and lemon juice. Set aside for 24 hours. Transfer to a large pan. Bruise the gingerroot, tie in a cheesecloth bag and add to the pan. Boil the fruit and gingerroot together for 15 minutes. Remove cheesecloth bag and add chopped crystallized ginger. Boil for another 5 minutes or until jellying point is reached, 220°-222° F on a jelly thermometer. Or dip a large spoon into the boiling mixture, let juice cool a bit, tilt the spoon and let juice drop back into the pan. If, as you tilt the spoon, the juice first separates into two distinct drops but then runs together and slides off the spoon in a sheet, the jellying point has been reached. Then pour into hot sterilized jars. Cover, seal and label. When cool, refrigerate. Use within a few weeks.

■  Quince Jelly

Quinces, the hard, woody fruit of the japonica, are difficult to cut up but pulp down quite easily. They have a delicate, subtle flavor.

Preparation and cooking time: 2 hours

4 pounds/2 kg quinces. 3¾ quarts/3 liters water.
2 teaspoons/10 ml citric acid. Sugar.

Wash the quinces. Cut up into small pieces and put into a large pot or canning kettle with 2½ quarts/2 liters of the water and the citric acid. Cover and simmer until tender, about 1 hour. Strain through several layers of cheesecloth or a jelly bag for 15 minutes. Reserve the liquid. Remove the pulp from the bag and cook again with the remaining 1¼ quarts/1 liter water for 30 minutes. Strain. Combine the two extracts. Measure and add ¾ cup sugar for each cup of juice. Heat until sugar dissolves, then boil until jellying point is reached, 220° – 222° F on a jelly thermometer. Or dip a large spoon into the boiling mixture, let juice cool a bit, tilt the spoon and let juice drop back into the pot. If, as you tilt the spoon, the juice first separates into two distinct drops but then runs together and slides off the spoon in a sheet, the jellying point has been reached. Then pour into hot sterilized jars and seal.

⊞ Grapefruit Curd

Any citrus fruit can be used to make a curd. Curds can be kept for only a month because of the egg and butter content.

Preparation and cooking time: ¾-1 hour

2 grapefruit. 2 eggs, beaten. 1 cup/200 g sugar. ½ cup/100 g butter.

Grate the peel of 1 grapefruit. Squeeze both grapefruit to extract the juice. Strain the juice into the top of a double boiler. Add the beaten eggs, grated peel, sugar and butter. Place over simmering water and cook until mixture thickens and coats the back of a spoon.
Pour into hot sterilized jars and seal.
When cool, refrigerate.

⊞ Dried Apricot Jam

A few blanched almonds added to the jam during simmering adds to the flavor. The nuts should be removed before pouring jam into jars.

Preparation and cooking time: 1½ hours and 24 hours

1 pound/500 g dried apricots. 2 quarts/1.5 liters water. Juice of 2 lemons. 6 cups/1.5 kg sugar.

Wash the apricots and soak in the water for 24 hours. Put the fruit and water in a pan, add the lemon juice and bring to a boil. Simmer for 30 minutes until the fruit is soft. Add the sugar and stir until it dissolves. Then boil rapidly, stirring frequently to prevent jam from sticking to the bottom of the pan, until jellying point is reached, 220°–222° F on a jelly thermometer. Or dip a large spoon into the boiling mixture, let juice cool a bit, tilt the spoon and let juice drop back into the pan. If, as you tilt the spoon, the juice separates into two distinct drops but then runs together and slides off the spoon in a sheet, the jellying point has been reached. Then pour into hot sterilized jars and seal. When cool, refrigerate. Use within a few weeks.

⊞ Apple Butter

If put up in small wide-mouthed jars, the butter can be turned out onto a plate and eaten with cream as a dessert.

Preparation and cooking time: 2 hours

1½ pounds/750 g (4 or 5 medium) cooking apples.
2½ cups/600 ml cider. Sugar. ½ teaspoon/2.5 ml cinnamon.

Wash and quarter apples but do not peel or core. Simmer the fruit with the cider until the apples become a pulp. Rub through a sieve. Measure the puree and add approximately ⅔ cup sugar for each cup of puree. Add cinnamon. Stir over low heat until sugar dissolves. Continue to stir frequently to prevent scorching. Bring to a boil and boil gently until mixture becomes thick and creamy. Pour into hot sterilized jars and seal. When cool, refrigerate. Use within a few weeks.

⊞ Melon and Ginger Jam

This is a very special jam with an unusual and intriguing flavor.

Preparation and cooking time: 1 hour and 24 hours

2½ cups/500 g diced melon. 2 cups/500 g sugar.
2 ounces (⅓ cup)/50 g chopped crystallized ginger.
Juice of 2 lemons.

Put melon in bowl with sugar and ginger. Cover and let stand overnight. Transfer to a heavy saucepan, add the lemon juice and simmer for 30 minutes – until melon looks transparent. Boil rapidly until jellying point is reached, 220° – 222° F on a jelly thermometer. Or dip a large spoon into the boiling mixture, let juice cool a bit, tilt the spoon and let juice drop back into the pan. If, as you tilt the spoon, the juice separates into two distinct drops but then runs together and slides off the spoon in a sheet, the jellying point has been reached. Then pour into hot sterilized jars and seal.
When cool, refrigerate. Use within a few weeks.

Strawberry Conserve

Soaking the fruit with the sugar has a hardening effect on the skins and so the fruit remains whole. Because of the relatively short cooking time, a conserve has a better color and flavor than strawberry jam.

Preparation and cooking time: 45 minutes and 3 days

4 pounds (2 heaping quarts or 15-16 cups)/ 2 kg perfect strawberries.
4 pounds (8 cups)/ 2 kg sugar.

Hull and then wipe the fruit. Layer the whole berries and sugar in a china or glass bowl. Let stand for 24 hours. Transfer the fruit and sugar to a canning kettle or large pot. Bring to a boil and boil for 5 minutes. Return mixture to bowl and let stand, covered, for a further 48 hours. Return to kettle and again bring to a boil. Boil for 10-20 minutes until jellying point is reached, 220°-222° F on a jelly thermometer. Or dip a large spoon into the boiling mixture, let juice cool a bit, tilt the spoon and let juice drop back into the kettle. If, as you tilt the spoon, the juice separates into two distinct drops but then runs together and slides off the spoon in a sheet, the jellying point has been reached. Then pour into hot sterilized jars and seal. When cool, refrigerate. Use within a few weeks.

Note: In England a special, large-crystal sugar called preserving sugar is available especially for this type of recipe. See the photograph of Strawberry Conserve. Ordinary granulated sugar will also produce satisfactory results.

Candied Peel

The syrup drained from the finished peel can be used as a syrup poured over fresh fruit desserts or for stewing fruit.

Preparation and cooking time: 2½ hours and 3 weeks

2 oranges. 2 lemons. 1¼ cups/300 ml water. 2 cups/500 g sugar.

Wash the fruit. Cut into quarters and peel. Simmer peel in a little water for 1½ hours until tender. Drain the peel. Reserve the liquid and add to it enough water to make 1¼ cups. Add 1 cup of the sugar and stir over low heat to dissolve. Then, slowly bring to a boil, pour over the peel and let stand for 2 days. Again, drain the peel. Reserve the syrup and add to it ½ cup of the sugar. Heat to dissolve the sugar and then bring to a boil. Pour over peel and let soak overnight. The next day, drain the peel and add the remaining ½ cup of the sugar to the syrup. Heat, dissolve the sugar and bring to a boil again. Pour over peel. Leave the peel in the thick syrup for 2 – 3 weeks. Drain and place peel on a flat dish. Let dry in a warm place. Store candied peel in airtight containers.

Fruit & Nut Conserve

An extravagant preserve but a little goes a long way. It makes an unusual filling for pies when mixed with other fruits such as apples or apricots.

Preparation and cooking time: 1½ hours

3 cups/650 g raisins. Grated peel and juice of 3 oranges.
Grated peel and juice of 1 lemon. 2 cups/200 g choppd walnuts.
2 cups/200 g chopped almonds. 2 cups/500 g sugar.
1¼ cups/300 ml pineapple juice.

Combine all the ingredients in a pan and simmer gently for 1 hour. Pour into hot sterilized jars and seal. When cool, refrigerate. Use within a few weeks.

Mincemeat

This is an old-fashioned, traditonal mincemeat. Keep it at least two weeks before using.

Preparation time: 1 hour

1 cup/225 g currants. 1 cup/225 g seedless white raisins.
1 cup/225 g raisins. 2 cups/225 g peeled, cored, grated apples.
½ cup/100 g chopped citrus peel. ¾ cup/100 g chopped blanched almonds.
1 cup/225 g dark brown sugar. 4 ounces/100 g suet, finely chopped.
1 tablespoon brandy (optional).
1 teaspoon/5 ml nutmeg. 1 teaspoon/5 ml cinnamon.
Peel of 1 lemon, cut up. Juice of 1 lemon.

Chop the currants and raisins and put in a bowl. Add the apples and citrus peel. Add all remaining ingredients. Stir well. Cover bowl and let stand for 2 days. Spoon into jars and cover. Refrigerate. Use within a few weeks.

◼ Spiced Clementines

Clementines are a small citrus fruit of the same family as tangerines.
They are delicious served as a garnish with cold duck, pork, ham or goose.

Preparation and cooking time: 1¼ hours

16 small clementines or tangerines. ½ teaspoon/2.5 ml baking soda.
12 whole allspice berries. 1 cinnamon stick. 1 small piece gingerroot.
12 whole cloves. 1¼ cups/300 ml white wine vinegar.
2 cups/500 g light brown sugar.

Wash the fruit and pierce a few holes in the skins with a toothpick or fine
skewer. Place in a large saucepan, add the baking soda and cover with
water. Bring to a boil and continue boiling for 12 minutes. Drain. Tie spices
in a cheesecloth bag. Add spices and vinegar to drained fruit in pan. Cover
and simmer for
20 minutes. Remove spice bag, add sugar and stir gently until it dissolves.
Simmer for 20 minutes more in covered pan. Using a slotted spoon, lift the
fruit gently and transfer to hot sterilized jars. Continue to simmer liquid for
another 10 minutes. Cool slightly and pour over fruit to fill jars. Seal the
jars and store in a refrigerator. Use within a few weeks.

Pickled Pears

Although pickled, pears keep their sweet flavor and are excellent served
with cold meats, particularly ham.

Preparation and cooking time: 30 minutes

1⅓ cups/500 g light corn syrup. 2 cups/450 ml vinegar.
¼ cinnamon stick. 8 whole cloves. 1 strip lemon peel.
3 pounds/1.5 kg pears.

Put all ingredients except pears in a saucepan and bring to a boil.
Let cool. Peel pears, leaving them whole, and put into sterilized jars. Strain
the cooled, spiced vinegar over the pears and seal. Refrigerate. Use
within a few weeks.

◼ PEARS IN BRANDY

Once opened, the fruit must be eaten within ten days. They will keep for
about a year with the seal unbroken.

Preparation and cooking time: 45 minutes

1½ cups/350 g sugar. 1¼ cups/300 ml water.
1 pound/500 g small pears. ⅔ cup/150 ml brandy.
5 or 6 cloves (optional).

Put sugar and water in a pan. Bring to a boil, stirring to dissolve the sugar.
Simmer for 10 minutes. Peel the pears but leave them whole. Put the
pears in the syrup and continue simmering for another
5 minutes. Remove pears with a slotted spoon and transfer to a large
sterilized jar. Simmer syrup for 5 more minutes; add brandy and cloves (if
used). Pour over the pears and seal. When cool, refrigerate. Do not
open for at least one month so that brandy may permeate the fruit.

◼ Potent Prunes

A really luxurious dessert when served with whipped cream.
The leftover syrup is delicious with ice cream.

Preparation and cooking time: 1½ hours

2 cups/500 g light brown sugar. 1¼ cups/300 ml cold tea.
1 pound/500 g dried prunes.
Brandy, port, sweet sherry or other sweet wine.

Put the sugar and cold tea together in a pan. Bring to the boiling point,
stirring all the while, and then simmer for 15 minutes. Add the prunes and
simmer for 40 minutes more. Remove prunes with a slotted spoon and
transfer to sterilized jars. Half-fill the jars with brandy or
wine and add syrup to fill jars. Seal jars.
When cool, refrigerate. Use within a few weeks.

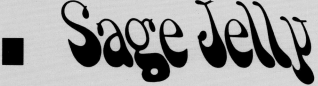

Sage Jelly

This is the ideal accompaniment for pork. Other herb jellies — mint or rosemary — can be made in the same way.

Preparation and cooking time: 1½ hours

3 pounds/1.5 kg (about 9) apples. Juice of 2 lemons.
Large bunch of fresh sage. Sugar. Green food color.

Wash and, without peeling or coring, cut up the apples. Put in a pan with just enough water to cover. Add the lemon juice. Simmer until fruit becomes a soft pulp. Strain through several layers of cheesecloth or a jelly bag. Finely chop the sage. Measure the apple juice and for each cup add ⅔ cup sugar. Heat the juice until the sugar dissolves and then boil rapidly for 5 minutes. Add the chopped sage and a few drops of green food color.

Boil until the jellying point is reached, 220°-222° F on a jelly thermometer. Or dip a large spoon into the boiling mixture, let juice cool a bit, tilt the spoon and let juice drop back into the pan. If, as you tilt the spoon, the juice separates into two distinct drops but then runs together and slides off the spoon in a sheet, the jellying point has been reached.

Pour into sterilized jars and cover.

◨Dried Apple Rings

Once dried, apple rings may be cooked by simmering gently in a little water sweetened with brown sugar or corn syrup.

Preparation and cooking time: 20 hours

Apples. ¼ cup/50 g salt.

Peel and core apples, removing all blemishes. Slice into rings ¼ inch thick. Put rings into a bowl of salted water to prevent discoloration. Remove rings from water and pat dry. Place on cookie sheets or thread on strings and tie to oven rack. Dry slowly in a cool oven for 4 – 6 hours. Temperature should not exceed 140° F. Remove from oven and let stand for 12 hours before packing in jars or containers.

◨ CRYSTALLIZED FLOWERS

Crystallized flowers keep their colors and shapes remarkably well — and look far too pretty to eat!

Preparation time: 30 minutes

1 egg white. 1 teaspoon/5 ml water. Sugar (preferably superfine). Small complete flowers such as the primrose, violet, freesia, pansy, or miniature rose — or rose petals or mint leaves.

Lightly beat the egg white and add water. Have sugar ready in a small, deep dish. With a small paint brush cover the upper surface of the flower lightly with the egg white mixture and then immerse flower in the sugar. Shake off surplus sugar and let flower dry overnight. Brush underside of flower with egg white mixture and dip again into sugar. Let flower dry and store carefully.

◻ *Raspberry Freezer Jam*

Because it is not a cooked preserve, this jam will not keep very long after defrosting.

Preparation time: 1½ hours and 48 hours

4½ cups/600 g raspberries. 4 cups/1 kg sugar.
4 fluid ounces/120 ml liquid pectin. 2 tablespoons/30 ml lemon juice.

Crush raspberries in a large bowl with a wooden spoon. Stir in the sugar and leave in a warm place for 1 hour. Stir frequently. Add liquid pectin and lemon juice and stir for 5 minutes until well mixed. Pour into small jars or plastic cups so that the jam is quickly used up once thawed. Cover with foil or airtight caps. Let stand in a warm kitchen for 48 hours. Label and freeze.

◼ RASPBERRY VINEGAR

Raspberry vinegar makes an excellent sweet and sour sauce for ice cream. Blackberries may be substituted for raspberries.

Preparation and cooking time: 30 minutes and 3 - 5 days

Ripe raspberries. Vinegar (preferably malt). Sugar.

For each 4 cups fruit, use 2½ cups vinegar. Combine in a china or glass bowl, cover with a clean cloth and let soak for 3-5 days. Strain off the liquid through several layers of cheesecloth or a jelly bag. For each cup liquid, add ⅔ cup sugar. Boil for 10 minutes. Pour into sterilized bottles and cork.

◻ *Syrup for Freezing*

Heavy syrup is suitable for soft fruits such as strawberries, black and red currants, raspberries and gooseberries. Medium syrup is used for freezing citrus fruits and fruits with pits, such as plums, apricots and peaches. Thin syrup is used for freezing apple slices.

Cooking time: 5 minutes

Heavy Syrup: 4 cups/1 kg sugar. 5 cups/1.25 liters water.
Medium Syrup: 2 cups/500 g sugar. 5 cups/1.25 liters water.
Thin Syrup: 1 cup/250 g sugar. 5 cups/1.25 liters water.

In a pan add sugar to water and heat gently, stirring until the sugar dissolves. Bring to a boil. Remove from heat and chill well before using.

■ Tomato Sauce

A very superior version of tomato catsup and useful to make when there is a surplus of tomatoes.

Preparation and cooking time: 2 hours

1 pound/500 g (4 medium) tomatoes.
½ pound/250 g (2 small) cooking apples. ⅔ cup/100 g chopped onions.
⅔ cup/150 ml vinegar (preferably malt). ½ cup/100 g sugar.
1 teaspoon/5 ml salt. 6 whole cloves. 2 pieces gingerroot.
12 peppercorns. 2 chilies.

Chop tomatoes and apples coarsely, including peels and cores. Place in a pan, add the onions, cover and simmer until soft. Add all the remaining ingredients and simmer, covered, for 30 minutes longer. Rub through a sieve and then return to pan. Simmer without lid for 15 minutes to thicken. Pour into hot sterilized jars, seal and place in a boiling water bath for 45 minutes. Label when cool.

Puddings

Gateau Amandine

Other flavorings may be added to the cream – soft fruits in season, crystallized ginger or chopped nuts.

Preparation and cooking time: 1½ hours

Sponge layers:
4 eggs. ¾ cup/150 g sugar. 1 cup/100 g flour.
Filling and decoration:
2 cups/450 ml heavy cream.
2 squares (1 oz. each)/50 g semisweet chocolate.
1 cup/100 g crumbled macaroons
(plus a few whole macaroons for decoration, if desired).

Preheat oven at 375° F. Prepare 6 cookie sheets by greasing and lining each with waxed paper and drawing an 8-inch-diameter circle on each. (Fewer cookie sheets may be used; reline the sheets before reusing.) Break eggs into a bowl, add the sugar and beat until mixture is thick and pale. (If beating is done by hand rather than electric mixer, this step must be done over hot water.) Carefully fold in the flour. Divide into 6 portions and spread on the circles marked on the waxed paper. Bake each layer for 5-8 minutes, until golden; peel off the paper and cool on a wire rack. For the filling, whip the cream until thick. Shave a few chocolate curls and reserve. Grate the remaining chocolate and fold it and the crumbled macaroons into the cream. Sandwich the sponge layers together with a filling of the flavored cream. Decorate the top with cream, chocolate curls and whole macaroons.

Crème Brulée

A really luxurious version of a baked egg custard, topped with crunchy toffee.

Preparation and cooking time: 45 minutes

1¼ cups/300 ml light cream. 1¼ cups/300 ml heavy cream.
4 egg yolks. ⅔ cup/125 g sugar. 6 drops vanilla. Sugar for topping.

Put both the light and heavy cream in the top of a double boiler and warm over simmering water. Beat egg yolks with 2 tablespoons of the sugar until pale-colored and thick. Pour into the warm cream and blend well. Add the vanilla. Continue to heat over hot water until mixture is thick enough to coat the back of a spoon. Strain into six broilerproof cups. Bake at 325° F for 8 minutes until a skin forms on the top. Refrigerate overnight. Three hours before serving, sprinkle the top of each cup liberally with sugar. Place under broiler briefly until sugar caramelizes. Chill again until ready to serve.

Wholemeal Treacle Tart

Just as good eaten hot or cold and a very good dessert for lunch boxes.

Preparation and cooking time: 45 minutes

6 tablespoons/75 g margarine. 1¼ cups/150 g whole wheat flour. 2 tablespoons/30 ml cold water. ⅓ cup/100 g light corn syrup. ⅓ cup/100 g dark molasses. 2 teaspoons/10 ml lemon juice. 1 rounded cup/50 g soft whole wheat bread crumbs.

Cut the margarine into the flour and bind together with cold water to form a ball of pastry dough. Roll out and line an 8-inch cake or pie pan with pastry. Combine the corn syrup, molasses and lemon juice and warm the mixture. Stir in the bread crumbs. Pour mixture into unbaked shell and, if desired, decorate with pastry trimmings. Bake at 425° F for 20 minutes.

Lincoln Tart

This is best served hot, straight from the oven, but it is also pleasantly chewy when eaten cold.

Preparation and cooking time: 35 minutes

¾ cup/150 g margarine. 1½ cups/150 g flour. Cold water. 3 tablespoons/90 ml jam. ¼ cup/50 g sugar. 1 tablespoon/25 g light corn syrup. 2 cups/150 g flaked coconut. 1 egg, beaten.

Cut half the margarine into the flour and add enough cold water to bind together and form into a ball. Roll out dough and line an 8-inch cake pan. (A pie or quiche pan will work equally well.) Spread the bottom with the jam. Combine remaining margarine, sugar and corn syrup in a saucepan and stir over low heat until margarine melts. Stir in coconut. Remove from heat and cool slightly. Add beaten egg. Spread this mixture over the jam and bake for about 25 minutes at 375° F.

CHESTNUT PARFAIT

A very rich dessert made even more sinfully delicious if you pass around a pitcher of light cream to pour over it.

Preparation and cooking time: 30 minutes

4 squares (1 oz. each)/100 g semisweet chocolate. ⅓ cup/75 g sugar. 5 tablespoons/75 ml water. 1 pound/450 g canned unsweetened chestnut puree. 2 eggs. ¾ cup/150 g butter, softened.

Combine the chocolate, sugar and water in a saucepan and heat slowly until chocolate melts and mixture is blended. Put the chestnut puree in a bowl and beat in the chocolate mixture. Separate the eggs and add the yolks to the bowl. Beat in the butter. Lightly beat the egg whites and then fold in. Turn the mixture into a mold and refrigerate overnight. Unmold, decorate if desired, and serve.

French Apple Flan

A beautiful golden-topped flan to serve at buffet parties.

Preparation and cooking time: 1¼ hours

6 tablespoons/75 g margarine. 1½ cups/150 g flour. Cold water. 1 pound/500 g (3 or 4) cooking apples. ⅓ cup/100 g light corn syrup. 2 teaspoons/10 ml lemon juice. ⅓ cup/100 g apricot jam.

Cut the margarine into the flour and bind together with enough cold water to form a ball of stiff pie dough. Roll out and line an 8-inch pan. Prick the pastry with a fork and bake the unfilled shell in a hot oven (450° F) for 10 − 15 minutes until crisp and brown. Peel, core and quarter the apples. Grate half the apple quarters. Mix the grated apples with corn syrup and lemon juice and spread on bottom of the baked pie shell. Slice remaining apple quarters very thin and arrange on top of grated fruit. Strain apricot jam and warm slightly. Brush over apples and bake at 350° F for 30 − 35 minutes.

■ SPOTTED RICHARD

Though occasionally addressed less formally, that is, as Spotted Dick,
this version of the famous pudding is too superior to be given
anything less than its proper title.
Preparation and cooking time: 2½ hours

1 cup/100 g flour. 1 teaspoon/5 ml baking powder. Cold water.
2½ cups/100 g soft white bread crumbs. 3 ounces/75 g suet, finely chopped.
½ cup/100 g chopped dates. ¼ cup/50 g mixed candied fruit peel.
¼ cup/50 g dark brown sugar. Corn syrup.

Sift together the flour and baking powder and add remaining
ingredients. Add enough cold water to make a soft dough. Turn out
onto a floured work surface and form into a sausage-shaped roll.
Wrap in waxed paper and then in a clean cloth. Tie cloth at both ends
(see picture). Either boil for 2 hours or steam for 2½ hours. Unwrap
pudding and cut into slices about ¾ inch thick. Arrange slices in a
circle on a serving dish. Warm corn syrup and pour over pudding.

■ PANCAKES

Two ways to make ordinary pancakes into super sweets!
Preparation and cooking time: 30 minutes

1 cup/100 g flour. Pinch salt. 1 egg. 1¼ cups/300 ml milk.
Unsalted butter. Juice of 1 orange or 1 lemon.
½ cup/100 g sugar or ⅓ cup/100 g light corn syrup.

Sift the flour and salt into a bowl. Make a well in the center. Break the
egg into the well. Stir from the center, gradually adding the milk as
you work in the flour. Beat for 1 minute and then allow batter to rest.
Melt a little butter in a frying pan. When hot, pour in a thin layer of
batter. When top surface bubbles, turn and cook on other side. Turn
the pancakes out onto a plate and serve sprinkled with orange or
lemon juice and with sugar or corn syrup. An alternative way is to
cook several pancakes and stack them with waxed paper between
each pancake. (They can also be frozen this way.) Then melt more
butter in the pan. Add orange or lemon juice and sugar or corn syrup.
When bubbling, put four pancakes folded into quarters into the pan
and simmer them in the sauce until heated through.
Serve with the sauce.

Claret Jelly

To make frosted grapes for decoration, as in the picture, brush the grapes with a little beaten egg and dip in sugar.

Preparation and cooking time: 30 minutes and 4 hours

1 envelope (1 tablespoon)/15 ml unflavored gelatin. 1 bottle red wine. 1 lemon. 1 small jar (8 oz.) red currant jelly. 1 cup/225 g sugar.

Soak the gelatin in ⅔ cup red wine. Peel the lemon as thin as possible. Squeeze the lemon to extract the juice. Put the remaining wine, lemon peel, lemon juice, red currant jelly and sugar in a saucepan and heat almost to the boiling point, stirring to dissolve the sugar. Remove from heat and stir in soaked gelatin. Stir to dissolve gelatin. Strain into individual serving glasses or a large bowl. Refrigerate until set. Decorate if desired.

☐ BANANAS TRINIDAD

For a children's dessert simply omit the flamed rum. Orange juice instead of lemon juice makes a delicious variation.

Preparation and cooking time: 30 minutes

2 tablespoons/25 g cornstarch. ⅔ cup/150 ml water.
2 tablespoons/30 ml lemon juice. ⅓ cup/100 g light corn syrup.
6 bananas. 2 tablespoons/25 g butter. 3 tablespoons/45 ml rum.

Blend the cornstarch with a little of the water in a saucepan. Add the rest of the water, lemon juice and corn syrup and cook over low heat, stirring constantly until the mixture thickens. Peel bananas. Cut each into lengthwise slices. Put in a buttered ovenproof dish. Cover with the sauce and dot with butter. Bake at 350° F for 20 minutes. Just before serving, sprinkle with rum and flame the rum.

☐ *Lemon Surprise Pudding*

When baked, the pudding separates into two layers, a light spongy topping and lemon sauce underneath.

Preparation and cooking time: 1 hour

1 large lemon. ¼ cup/50 g butter. ½ cup/100 g sugar. 2 eggs.
½ cup/50 g self-rising flour. 1¼ cups/300 ml milk.

Grate the lemon peel and squeeze the lemon to extract the juice. Cream the butter, sugar and grated lemon peel together until pale-colored and soft. Separate the eggs and beat the yolks and half the flour into the mixture. Gradually stir in the milk and the lemon juice and beat in the remaining flour. Beat the egg whites until stiff and fold in. Pour into a
1½ quart ovenproof dish and bake at 350° F for 40 minutes.

☐ Meringue Baskets

The baskets can be filled with fresh fruit and cream. The meringue mixture can be made into one large basket rather than smaller ones.

Preparation and cooking time: 2-3 hours

4 egg whites. 1 cup/225 g sugar.

Line a large cookie sheet with waxed paper and brush lightly with oil. Preheat oven at 200° F. Beat the egg whites until very stiff. Add half the sugar and continue beating until whites hold peaks. Fold in the remaining sugar. Divide one-third of the mixture into 4 to 6 circles on the waxed paper. Pipe the rest of the meringue around the edge of each circle to form the sides of each basket. Bake for 2 – 3 hours until crisp and dry. Meringue baskets may be stored for up to one month in airtight containers.

◨ Apricot & Almond Charlotte

Apricots and nuts make for a more exciting version of the usual fruit charlotte.

Preparation and cooking time: 45 minutes

Butter. 6 slices buttered bread, cut into finger-size strips.
1 can (16 oz.)/452 g apricot halves. ½ cup/50 g chopped almonds.
¾ cup/150 g light brown sugar.

Butter a small round baking dish suitable for a deep-dish pie. Line with strips of the buttered bread, buttered side out. Drain the apricots, reserving 5 ounces of the juice. Layer the apricots, almonds and ½ cup/100g of the brown sugar in the dish. Pour over the apricot juice. Cover the top of the dish with more bread strips buttered side up, and sprinkle with the remaining brown sugar. Bake at 400° F for 30 minutes until crisp on top.

◨ CARAMELIZED ORANGES

Thin slivers of toasted almonds sprinkled on top of the oranges add a nice finishing touch.

Preparation and cooking time: 45 minutes

8 oranges. 1 cup/250 g sugar. 1¼ cups/300 ml water.

Remove the outer layer of peel from 2 of the oranges. Cut this peel into narrow strips and plunge into boiling water for 5 minutes. Drain and rinse in cold water. Set aside. Peel the remaining oranges and remove all traces of white skin from all the fruit. Cut crosswise slices, removing any seeds, Once sliced, reassemble each orange and fasten slices together with toothpicks. Put the sugar and half the water in a saucepan. Dissolve the sugar over low heat and then bring to a boil. Continue boiling until the color changes to a golden brown. Remove the pan from heat and immediately pour in the rest of the water, being careful not to splash any. Heat again slowly to dissolve the caramel. Remove from heat. When cold, pour over the oranges and garnish with the strips of peel.

◨ Pineapple Upside-Down Cake

A colorful dessert, good either hot or cold.

Preparation and cooking time: 1¼ hours

Topping:
⅓ cup plus 1 tablespoon/75 g dark brown sugar.
6 tablespoons/75 g margarine.
1 can (15 oz./350 g) sliced pineapple, drained.
Maraschino or candied cherries, cut in half.
Cake:
½ cup/100 g margarine. ½ cup/100 g granulated sugar.
2 eggs. 1 cup/100 g self-rising flour.

For the topping, cream together the brown sugar and margarine and spread all over the base of an 8-inch round cake pan. Arrange the pineapple slices on top and place a half-cherry in the center of each. Prepare the cake batter by creaming together the margarine and the granulated sugar until light and soft. Beat in the eggs. Sift and fold in the flour. Carefully pour over pineapple and spread evenly. Bake at 350° for 45 – 50 minutes. Let stand 5 minutes before turning upside down onto serving plate.

◨ PEACH CONDÉ

Canned rice pudding can be used for a hurry-up dessert.

Preparation and cooking time: 1 hour

⅓ cup/50 g short-grain rice. 2½ cups/600 ml milk. ¼ cup/50 g sugar.
Few drops vanilla. 6 canned peach halves. Fruit drink.
4 teaspoons/25 g arrowroot.
Yellow food color (optional).

Wash the rice and simmer with the milk until thick and creamy. Let cool. Stir in sugar and vanilla. Divide into 6 serving dishes. Drain canned peaches, reserving syrup, and put one peach half on each dish, round side up. Measure the syrup and add enough fruit drink to make 1¼ cups. Heat the liquid with the arrowroot gently until thickened. Add color if desired. Pour sauce over the fruit and allow to set for a few minutes.

Note: this dessert may be made with fresh peaches. Peel 3 peaches and cut each in half, putting one half on each dish. Make sauce by thickening 1¼ cups fruit drink with arrowroot.

Gateau St Honoré

This fabulous gâteau is one of the classic French pâtisseries.

Preparation and cooking time: 1¼ hours

Rich pastry:
6 tablespoons/75 g butter. 1½ cups/150 g flour.
¼ cup/25 g confectioners' sugar. 1 egg yolk. Cold water.
Choux pastry:
½ cup/100 g butter. 1¼ cups/300 ml water.
1 cup plus 2 tablespoons/125 g flour. 4 eggs.
Filling:
Sweetened whipped cream or crème pâtissière
(for a crème pâtissière recipe, see filling for Vanilla Slice).
Caramel:
1 cup/200 g granulated sugar. ¼ cup/60 ml water.

To prepare the rich pastry, cut the butter into the flour, stir in the confectioners' sugar and bind together with the egg yolk and about 2 teaspoons/10 ml cold water. Form into a ball. Roll out and cut a circle 8 inches in diameter. Transfer to a greased cookie sheet. To make the choux pastry, over low heat melt the butter in the water, then add the flour and beat mixture over low heat until a soft ball forms. Remove from heat and beat in the eggs one at a time. Transfer to a pastry bag and pipe a ring of choux pastry around the edge of the rich pastry circle already on the cookie sheet. Then pipe the rest into small balls on a separate greased cookie sheet. Bake both sheets at 400° F for 30 minutes. Cool and fill the circular pastry base with sweetened whipped cream filling. Make caramel by dissolving the sugar in the water and boiling until a pale golden color. Dip each choux ball in the caramel and fix in place around the border of the gâteau with a little more cream. The remaining caramel can be spun into threads for more decoration.

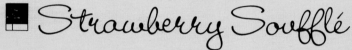

Strawberry Soufflé

Any soft fruit that is available can be used instead of strawberries.

Preparation and cooking time: 45 minutes

2 pounds (2 heaping pints or about 7 cups)/1 kg strawberries.
1 envelope (1 tablespoon)/15 ml unflavored gelatin.
4 tablespoons/60 ml water. 1¼ cups/250 g sugar.
Juice of 2 lemons, strained. 3 egg whites. 1¼ cups/300 ml heavy cream.

Tie a collar of foil or a double layer of waxed paper around a 1-quart soufflé dish. Wash and hull berries. Reserve a few berries for decoration and press the others through a sieve or liquify in a blender. Soak the gelatin in the water. Put half of the fruit puree in a pan, add ¾ cup/150 g of the sugar, the gelatin and the lemon juice. Stir gently over low heat until sugar and gelatin dissolve. Remove from heat and add other half of the puree. Let cool. Beat egg whites until stiff, adding remaining sugar. Whip the cream until thick. Fold both egg whites and whipped cream into strawberry mixture and blend well. Pour into prepared soufflé dish and refrigerate until firm. Carefully remove collar and decorate before serving.

Toffee Apple Pudding

The pudding has a toffee-tasting topping.

Preparation and cooking time: 2½ hours

1 large cooking apple. ⅓ cup/100 g light corn syrup. ¾ cup/150 g margarine.
¾ cup/150 g sugar. 3 eggs. 1½ cups/150 g self-rising flour.

Grease a large mold. Peel, core and slice the apple. Arrange the slices on the bottom of the mold and pour the corn syrup over them. Cream the margarine and sugar until pale-colored and soft. Beat the eggs and add them gradually, mixing well. Fold in the flour. Spread the batter over the apples. Cover the mold with waxed paper or foil and wrap in a clean cloth. Place on a trivet in a heavy kettle over boiling water. Cover. Steam for 2 hours, adding water to the kettle if necessary, until sponge mixture is cooked. Turn out onto a warm plate and serve with additional corn syrup or custard sauce.

Rhubarb and Orange Fool

A cool summer dessert. Serve it with thin, crisp ginger snaps.

Preparation and cooking time: 45 minutes

1 pound/500 g rhubarb. 1 large orange. ⅓ cup/100 g light corn syrup.
Red food color (optional). 1¼ cups/300 ml heavy cream or thick custard.

Wash the rhubarb and cut into 1-inch pieces. There should be 3 cups. Grate the orange peel and squeeze the fruit to extract the juice. Gently stew the rhubarb with the orange peel, orange juice and corn syrup until tender. Puree the rhubarb in a blender or press through a sieve. Let cool. Whip the cream until thick. Blend the puree into the cream and add a few drops of red food color if desired. Pour into individual serving glasses or a large bowl. Decorate.

BLACKBERRY MOUSSE

Fruit mousses are economical desserts to make when summer fruits are a little overripe.

Preparation and cooking time: 45 minutes

2 cups/250 g blackberries. ¼ cup/50 g sugar.
½ envelope (1½ teaspoons)/7 ml unflavored gelatin.
1 small can (5 oz.) evaporated milk. 2 egg whites.

Wash the blackberries and put them in a pan along with the sugar. Cover and cook until tender. Press through a sieve. Sprinkle the gelatin over the warm puree and stir until dissolved. Whip the evaporated milk until thick. Beat the egg whites until stiff. Fold the milk and the egg whites into the puree. Pour into a serving dish and chill until set.

Whiskey and Oatmeal Syllabub

This is not a traditional syllabub but it is an impressive pudding to serve after a perfect dinner.

Preparation time: 20 minutes

⅓ cup/25 g steel-cut oatmeal. 1¼ cups/300 ml heavy cream.
⅓ cup/100 g light corn syrup. 5 tablespoons/75 ml Scotch whiskey.
1 teaspoon/5 ml lemon juice.

Toast the oatmeal under the broiler until golden brown. Whip the cream until stiff. Mix together corn syrup, whiskey and lemon juice. Fold into the cream. Reserve 1 or 2 spoonfuls of oatmeal. Fold the rest into the cream. Pile into glasses and chill. Sprinkle with remaining oatmeal before serving. *Note:* this recipe may be prepared with rolled oats although the texture will be slightly different.

RASPBERRY MOUSSE MOLD

The flavor of the meringues can be varied by adding chopped filberts to the mixture.

Preparation and cooking time: 30 minutes and 1½ hours

12 ounces (3 cups)/375 g fresh or frozen raspberries.
1 cup/100 g confectioners' sugar.
½ envelope (1½ teaspoons)/ 7 ml unflavored gelatin.
2 tablespoons/30 ml hot water. 1 egg, separated.
1 small can (5 oz.) evaporated milk
Meringue:
1 egg white. ¼ cup/50 g granulated sugar.

Crush the raspberries, add the confectioners' sugar and mix. Dissolve the gelatin in the hot water and then stir into the raspberry mixture along with the egg yolk. Beat the evaporated milk until foamy and fold into the mixture. Beat the egg white until stiff and fold in. Pour the mixture into a mold or bowl and chill. Prepare the meringue by beating the egg white until stiff. Add the granulated sugar and beat until very stiff. Put into pastry bag or tube and pipe out into small stars on a greased, waxed-paper-lined cookie sheet. Bake at 250° F for 1½-2 hours. Carefully unmold mousse onto serving dish and cover with meringue stars.

■ Sussex Pond Pudding

During cooking, the lemon inside the pudding bursts and produces a
delicious lemon sauce. Each serving should include a
piece of the lemon.

Preparation and cooking time: 2½ hours

*1¾ cups/225 g self-rising flour. 4 ounces/100 g suet, finely chopped.
Pinch salt. Cold water. ¾ cup/150 g light brown sugar.
¾ cup/150 g butter. 1 large lemon. 2 tablespoons/30 ml water.*

Mix the flour, suet and salt in a bowl. Add enough cold water to make
a soft dough. Form into a ball. Grease an ovenproof bowl. Reserve
about a quarter of the dough. Roll out the remaining dough into a
circle large enough to line the bowl. Sprinkle half the sugar over the
dough lining the bowl and then cut up half the butter and mix it with
the sugar in the bowl. Prick the lemon all over with a darning needle
or very fine skewer and put on top of sugar and butter in dish. Cover
the lemon with the remaining sugar and butter.

Add the 2 tablespoons/30 ml water. Roll out the reserved dough into
a circle that will fit on top of the pudding. Seal this 'lid' to the dough
lining the bowl. Cover the bowl with waxed paper or foil and wrap in a
clean cloth. Place on a trivet in a heavy kettle over boiling water.
Cover. Steam for 2 hours, adding water to the kettle if necessary.

MINCEMEAT AND APPLE JALOUSIE

Jalousie is the name given to the shutters of French houses. The dessert should look rather like these shutters when it is baked.

Preparation and cooking time: 1 hour

8 ounces/250 g frozen puff pastry dough. ¾ cup/250 g mincemeat. ½ pound/250 g (about 2 small) cooking apples. ½ cup/100 g dark brown sugar. Confectioners' sugar.

Roll out the puff pastry to an oblong approximately 12 inches by 10 inches. Cut into 2 wide strips – one slightly wider than the other. Put the narrower one on a greased cookie sheet and spread with mincemeat, leaving a 1-inch margin at each edge. Peel, core and slice the apples and arrange on top of the mincemeat. Sprinkle brown sugar over the apples. Fold the remaining strip of pastry in half lengthwise and, using kitchen shears, snip along the folded edge at ½-inch intervals, cutting to within 1 inch of the outside edge. Unfold. With cold water wet all 4 edges of the pastry on the cookie sheet. Carefully put the cut strip on top and press together edges of top and bottom strips to seal.
Bake at 375° for 30 minutes. Sprinkle with confectioners' sugar before serving.

Baked Ginger Pears

A drop or two of yellow food color in the poaching syrup will brighten the color of cooked pears.

Preparation and cooking time: 30 minutes

8 small cooking pears. ⅔ cup/150 ml water. ½ cup/100 g sugar. 1 teaspoon/5 ml ginger. Few strips lemon peel. ½ cup/50 g slivered almonds.

Peel the pears, leaving them whole and with stems still on. Combine water, sugar, ginger and lemon peel in a saucepan and bring to a boil. Stir to dissolve sugar. Add pears and poach gently until tender. Remove pears carefully. Stud with slivered almonds. Let cool and refrigerate. Serve cold in a glass bowl with the syrup.

Lemon and Grape Cheesecake

The sweet crunchiness of the grapes makes an exciting contrast with the creamy filling.

Preparation and cooking time: 45 minutes

Graham cracker crust:
2½ cups/225 g graham cracker crumbs.
½ cup/100 g butter. 1 tablespoon/25 g light corn syrup.
Filling:
2 small packages (3 oz. each)/150 g cream cheese.
¼ cup/50 g sugar. 2 eggs, separated. Grated peel and juice of 1 lemon.
½ envelope (1½ teaspoons)/7 ml unflavored gelatin.
2 tablespoons/30 ml hot water. ⅔ cup/150 ml plain yogurt.
⅔ cup/150 ml heavy cream.
Decoration:
Black and green grapes, seeded and cut in half.

Over low heat, melt the butter. Stir in the corn syrup. Remove from heat and add the graham cracker crumbs. Toss until well blended. Press onto bottom and along inside of an 8-inch springform pan, forming a crust. Let stand in a cool place to set. For the filling, beat the cream cheese and sugar together until soft and creamy. Add the egg yolks, grated lemon peel and lemon juice. Soften the gelatin in the hot water and stir into the cheese mixture. Add the yogurt. Whip the cream until thick and fold in. Beat the egg whites until stiff and fold in. Pour into the graham cracker crust and refrigerate until set. Decorate with grapes, remove the springform side and serve.

⊞ Praline Ice Cream

Praline is a brittle toffee made with sugar and chopped almonds. (Look for the recipe in this book.)

Preparation and freezing time: 3 hours

1¼ cups/300 ml heavy cream. 2 egg yolks.
½ cup/50 g confectioners' sugar. 6 drops vanilla.
¾ cup/100 g crushed praline.

Whip the cream until thick but not stiff. Mix egg yolks and sugar together and fold into cream along with vanilla. Pour into a bowl or plastic container and freeze. About an hour before serving transfer the ice cream from the freezing compartment to the refrigerator so it will not be rock hard when served. Just before serving stir in the crushed praline. (The praline has a high sugar content and would not freeze if added to the ice cream in the initial mixture.)

⊞ RUM STOCKADE

This pudding is rather rich and the combination of rum and chocolate makes it an especially tempting treat.

Preparation time: 30 minutes

Ladyfingers. 4 tablespoons/60 ml rum. ½ cup/100 g butter.
½ cup/75 g sugar. 4 squares (1 oz. each)/100 g semisweet chocolate.
2 eggs. Chocolate curls (optional).

Dip the ladyfingers in rum and arrange around the inside of a soufflé dish or a round mold approximately 6 inches in diameter. Cream together butter and sugar. Melt the chocolate over hot water and stir into the butter-sugar mixture. Separate eggs and add the yolks to the mixture. Beat the whites until stiff and fold in, along with any remaining rum. Pour into the center of the circle of ladyfingers and refrigerate for 24 hours. Turn out onto a serving plate and decorate with chocolate curls if desired.

⊞ SWISS APPLE

An easy pudding which children will love.

Preparation and cooking time: 30 minutes

1 pound/500 g (about 3 medium) cooking apples.
⅓-½ cup/75-100 g sugar. 1 teaspoon water.
1¼ cups/300 ml heavy cream.
2-3 tablespoons/50 g light corn syrup. 2 cups/50 g cornflakes.

Peel, core and quarter the apples. Simmer with the sugar and the water until they are a soft pulp. Beat well until smooth. Divide equally among 4-6 serving dishes. Let cool. Whip the cream and spread over the apple mixture. Warm the corn syrup in a pan and stir in the cornflakes. When they are well coated, spoon onto cream and serve.

⊞ BROWN BREAD PUDDING

An old-fashioned winter pudding, delicious served with real custard sauce.

Preparation and cooking time: 2½ hours

5 cups/225 g soft whole wheat or other brown bread crumbs.
¼ bottle (about ¾ cup/200 ml) white wine. ½ cup/100 g light brown sugar.
½ teaspoon/2.5 ml cinnamon. ½ teaspoon/2.5 ml nutmeg.
1 cup/100 g dried fruit. ¼ cup/50 g butter. 2 eggs. Milk.

Soak the bread crumbs in the wine for 30 minutes. Mix in the sugar, spices and dried fruit. Melt the butter and pour in. Beat the eggs and add, mixing well. If consistency is not soft, mix in a little milk. Put mixture into a buttered pan or pie plate and bake at 325° F for 1¼ – 1½ hours until crisp and golden.

■ Butterscotch Meringue Pie

Light-textured and delicious, particularly when served hot from the oven.

Preparation and cooking time: 1½ hours

½ cup/50 g flour. ½ cup/100 g dark brown sugar. ¾ cup/200 ml milk. ¼ cup/50 g butter. 1 teaspoon/5 ml vanilla. 3 eggs, separated. 1 baked 8-inch flan, quiche or pie shell. ¾ cup/150 g granulated sugar.

Blend together the flour and brown sugar in a small saucepan. Gradually stir in the milk and heat to the boiling point. Remove from heat and beat in butter and vanilla. Beat the egg yolks into the pan and pour mixture into shell. Beat the egg whites until they begin to form soft peaks. Add half the granulated sugar and continue beating until peaks are stiff and glossy. Fold the rest of the granulated sugar into the egg whites and beat until very stiff. Heap the meringue on top of the butterscotch filling. Bake at 275° F for 30 — 45 minutes until golden brown.